First published in 2007 by New Holland Publishers (UK) Ltd
London • Cape Town • Sydney • Auckland
Garfield House, 86–88 Edgware Road, London W2 2EA, United Kingdom
www.newhollandpublishers.com
80 McKenzie Street, Cape Town 8001, South Africa
14 Aquatic Drive, Frenchs Forest, NSW 2086, Australia
218 Lake Road, Northcote, Auckland
Copyright © 2007 text AG&G Books
The right of David Squire to be identified as author of this work has been asserted by him in
accordance with the Copyright, Designs and Patents Act 1988.
Copyright © 2007 illustrations and photographs New Holland Publishers (UK) Ltd
Copyright © 2007 New Holland Publishers (UK) Ltd
ISBN 978 1 84537 485 3
10 9 8 7 6 5 4 3 2 1
Editorial Direction: Rosemary Wilkinson Editor: Anne Konopelski Production: Hazel Kirkman
Designed and created for New Holland by AG&G Books Copyright © 2004 "Specialist" AG&G Books
Design: Glyn Bridgewater Illustrations: Dawn Brend, Gill Bridgewater, Coral Mula and Ann Winterbotham
Editor: Alison Copland Photographs: see page 80
Reproduction by Pica Digital Pte Ltd, Singapore
Printed and bound in Malaysia by Times Offset (M) Sdn. Bhd.
The information in this book is true and complete to the best of our knowledge. All recommendations
are made without guarantee on the part of the authors and the publishers. The authors and publishers
disclaim any liability for damages or injury resulting from the use of this information.

The Garden
PESTS & DISEASES
Specialist

The essential guide to identifying
and controlling pests and diseases of
ornamentals, vegetables and fruits

David Squire
Series editors: A. & G. Bridgewater

NH
NEW HOLLAND

Contents

Author's foreword 2

Author's foreword

If left untreated, pests and diseases soon wreak havoc in gardens, especially in flower borders, vegetable plots and fruit areas where plants with a similar nature are grown massed together. These plants provide a ready menu for both pests and diseases. The sooner such outbreaks are treated, the easier it is to eradicate them, especially when trying to control aphids, which reproduce rapidly if controls are neglected.

Identifying pests and diseases is not always easy, and many initially affect the undersides of leaves and cannot readily be seen. Some live in the soil and their presence only becomes apparent when plants wilt after their roots or stems have been chewed.

This highly illustrated and easy-to-use book groups plants – such as roses, border flowers, container-grown types, water plants, culinary herbs, soft fruits, tree fruits, vegetables and houseplants –

and shows the range of pests and diseases that attack them. Physiological disorders are also included. This enables the problem to be readily identified and the right control or preventative measure to be adopted.

In addition to using chemicals, many pests can be controlled by encouraging beneficial insects – as well as frogs, toads and hedgehogs – into gardens, and this should always be the first consideration, especially as it is an inexpensive and environmentally friendly way to keep plants clean and healthy.

Measurements

Both metric and imperial measurements are given in this book – for example, 1.8 m (6 ft).

SEASONS

Throughout this book, advice is given about the times to spray or dust plants, should this be necessary. Because of global and even regional variations in climate and temperature, the four main seasons have been used, with each subdivided into 'early', 'mid-' and 'late' – for example, early spring, mid-spring and late spring. These 12 divisions of the year can be applied to the appropriate calendar months in your local area, if you find this helpful.

Caution

When using chemicals in gardens, whether as sprays, dusts or baits, take care that they do not contact your skin or eyes. Also ensure that domestic animals cannot lick or chew newly sprayed plants, and check that wild animals cannot gain access to baits. Always treat garden chemicals with respect. Wherever practical, collected pests and infected plant material should be destroyed by burning.

Range of pests and diseases

Plant pests and diseases come in a great many shapes and forms, and they can cause damage to every part of a plant, from roots and stems to flowers and fruits. The term 'pest' encompasses insects, such as aphids and beetles, as well as mites, slugs and snails. 'Diseases' include viruses. There are also cultural problems, or physiological disorders, such as scorched leaves, to consider; these are caused by unsuitable growing conditions.

What do they damage?

WHAT IS AN INSECT?

A typical insect has a body formed of three parts (head, thorax and abdomen), with three pairs of legs attached to the thorax. Most insects have a life cycle comprising egg, larva (commonly known as caterpillar, grub or maggot), pupa (chrysalis) and adult, and this is known as a complete metamorphosis. Other insects may have an incomplete metamorphosis, with no true pupal stage.

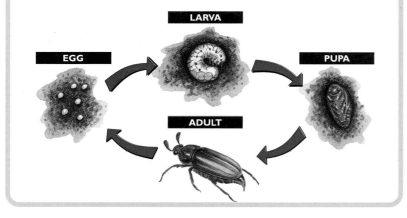

EGG — LARVA — PUPA — ADULT

TYPICAL DAMAGE

Insects (as well as pests that are not true insects) that cause damage can, in general terms, be described as those that bite or chew leaves, stems and flowers, those that pierce and suck sap from plants, and those that burrow into leaves, often creating ribbons of damage.

Biting or chewing pests include beetles, caterpillars, earwigs, millipedes, woodlice, slugs and snails.

Sucking pests include aphids, blackfly, thrips, capsid bugs and whitefly.

Burrowing or leaf-mining pests include chrysanthemum leaf miner and chrysanthemum eelworm.

What is a mite?

These are minute, spider-like pests, with four pairs of legs and mouthparts that enable them to pierce the foliage and to suck sap, causing mottling, yellowing, wilting and discoloration. Flowers are also attacked. They infest many plants, including those in greenhouses as well as ornamental plants outdoors, and fruit trees and bushes.

Red spider mites

WHAT ARE DISEASES?

There are several types that affect plants:
- **Fungal diseases:** Mainly parasitical, with the fungus feeding on the host plant. Well-known ones include damping off on seedlings (encouraged by damp and badly ventilated greenhouses) and black spot on roses.
- **Bacterial diseases:** Individual bacteria are some of the smallest living organisms. Examples of them in plants include blackleg of potatoes, crown gall and gladiolus scab.
- **Rusts:** Type of fungus that produces rust-red or brown, raised areas on leaves, such as when infecting carnations.
- **Viruses:** Live in the sap of plants, stunting and deforming growth; mainly spread by sap-sucking insects and when infected plants are propagated.

Soil and rubbish pests

There are many pests that live in the soil and attack the roots of plants, and these include wireworms and leatherjackets. Some pests hide under garden rubbish and come out at night.

Cultural problems

Sometimes known as physiological disorders, they are encouraged by unsuitable environmental factors or cultivation disorders. They include scalding in grapes and sun scald on tomatoes.

OTHER PESTS

Many plant-damaging pests are not insects, and these include slugs and snails, millipedes and woodlice. These pests often attack plants at night and hide under rubbish or in the soil during the day. For this reason, remove and burn all rubbish.

Prevention and control

Is prevention better than control?

Whenever possible, it is far better to prevent a pest or disease attack than to have to eradicate it later, when it is established and causing a major problem. Increasingly, controlling pests and diseases 'organically', without having to resort to chemicals, is considered to be the best policy, not only for the good of the environment but also for the welfare of you and your family. It will also help to achieve a natural 'balance' in your garden.

Leaves of brassicas, such as cabbages and broccoli, are often badly damaged by pigeons and other birds.

Ladybirds multiply rapidly in summer and are voracious eaters of pests such as aphids, mites and thrips.

Chemical controls

Dealing with insects
There are two types of chemicals used to kill insects and other pests — 'contact' and 'systemic'.

- **Contact insecticide:** Sprayed at the first sign of a pest attack, it kills the insect by contact or by making the plant's surface toxic.
- **Systemic insecticide:** Chemicals enter a plant's sap and make it toxic to insects.

Dealing with diseases
Similarly, there are two types of chemicals used to prevent and control diseases — 'contact' and 'systemic'.

- **Contact fungicide:** Sprayed on plants anticipated to be infected by a disease, it kills germinating fungal spores and prevents further infection. However, it has little effect on established fungal growths.
- **Systemic fungicide:** Absorbed by the plant, it enters the sap stream, where it is able to kill fungi within the plant's tissue.

General prevention

There are many easy and general ways to keep plants healthy.

- **Balanced plant foods:** Where plants are predominantly fed nitrogen, it creates soft, sappy growth that is vulnerable to pests and diseases. Nitrogen, potash and phosphate, as well as minor and trace elements, need to be in balance.
- **Cleaning greenhouses:** In early winter, remove all plants and scrub the inside. Then, leave the doors and ventilators open for several weeks.
- **Growing houseplants:** Always use clean compost and pots.
- **Hoeing:** Disturbing the soil's surface throughout summer both kills weeds and discourages soil pests.
- **Removing all weeds:** Many weeds offer homes to pests and diseases and should be pulled up and burned. If left among cultivated plants, they also reduce the flow of air and encourage dampness.
- **Rotating crops:** Each year, rotate crops in a vegetable plot. This helps to prevent the build-up of pests and diseases.
- **Sowing seeds in greenhouses:** Sow thinly and avoid both low temperatures and high humidity.
- **Sowing seeds outdoors:** Sow thinly and evenly. Congested seedlings are wasteful of money and encourage the presence of diseases.
- **Vegetable plots:** Every year, dig the soil to bury weeds and to incorporate well-decomposed manure or vegetable waste. Digging it also exposes soil pests to frost and birds.

Non-chemical methods for specific plants

There are many ways to deter the presence of pests; here are a few, but others are described throughout this book (see also pages 76–77).

- **Carrot root fly** are attracted to carrots by their strong smell. Strips of paraffin (kerosene)-soaked rags placed between rows of carrots help to confuse carrot fly. Lawn mowings can also be used.

- **Greenhouse red spider mites** can be deterred by mist-spraying plants in the morning and early afternoon; allow excessive moisture to evaporate by nightfall.

- **Moles** disturb the soil with their tunnels and mounds. They can be deterred by planting 'repellent' plants such as *Euphorbia lathyrus* (Caper Spurge) near mole runs.

Euphorbia lathyrus (Caper Spurge)

Beneficial insects

In nature, there is always a balance – at one moment an insect can be ravenously munching leaves or sucking sap, while a few seconds later it can become another pest's supper. There are some beneficial pests that are slightly more sophisticated, and instead of just eating a foe they lay eggs in it so that their young, when hatched, have a ready source of food. These are known as parasitical beneficial insects, whereas those that just eat their prey are predators.

Ladybirds are popular and attractive predators, eating vast numbers of aphids, as well as mites, thrips, mealy bugs and scale insects.

Ladybirds, as well as many other predatory and parasitical beneficial insects, are illustrated and described on pages 6–7.

The names for ladybirds vary widely and include 'ladyfly' and 'ladycow'. 'Cushcow lady', another name said to mean 'bird or beetle of Our Lady', is claimed to have arisen because of the wonderful service the ladybird performs by eating vast numbers of greenfly.

Warning: Ladybirds, as well as other beneficial insects, are quickly killed by the use of chemical sprays.

Other beneficial creatures

Many beneficial creatures are featured on pages 6–7; several are naturally present, such as centipedes (especially if a garden is not clinically tidy), while others can be encouraged into gardens, particularly if a wildlife garden pond is present.

Gardening, especially growing large numbers of the same type of plant close together, encourages a build-up of pests, ultimately to a level when beneficial insects are unable to control them. Gardeners are usually unaware that they have upset the balance of nature between one insect and another.

Where garden plants have been regularly sprayed with insecticides over several years, this greatly reduces the number of beneficial insects and creatures, as well as radically delaying their return when spraying with chemicals stops.

Hedgehogs feed at night, on slugs, earwigs, millipedes, caterpillars and beetles. The European hedgehog lives up to 5–6 years.

Hedgehogs roam over large distances in search of food

Biological controls in greenhouses

Bacterial diseases can be used to kill caterpillars

Commercial greenhouses – as well as domestic types when packed with enthusiast's plants including orchids and food crops like tomatoes – offer plant pests a concentrated source of food. During recent years, a wide range of biological controls using parasites and predators, as well as bacterial diseases, have been used to control pests in the enclosed environments of greenhouses. However, in general they need good light and a temperature of 21°C (70°F) to breed rapidly and at a rate that exceeds that of the pests.

A range of biological controls in greenhouses is featured on page 7; when using them, stop using pesticides, although insecticidal soaps (which control many mites and small insects) can still be used.

ORGANIC GARDENING

About 60 years ago, there began to be an increased reliance on the use of chemicals in the pursuit of high yields for food crops and keeping garden and greenhouse plants healthy. The philosophy of relying on chemicals was initially embraced by commercial growers and home gardeners, but during recent decades the prevention and control of pests and diseases, as well as a reluctance to resort to fertilizers with residues that poison land and watercourses, has come to be accepted as the right way to grow plants. It is known as organic or green gardening (see 'Getting the terms right …' on page 6 for definitions).

Many home gardeners endeavour to grow food crops – ranging from vegetables and culinary herbs to fruits – that are uncontaminated with pesticides and fungicides, and avoid the use of unnatural fertilizers. Organic gardening demands more involvement with plants than just using a spray to eradicate pests. Therefore, you should be prepared to get to know plants and pests in greater detail.

Biological controls

What are biological controls?

The term 'biological control' refers to the control of plant-damaging pests through the use of certain insects that act as predators or parasites. Other creatures such as centipedes, hedgehogs, frogs and toads can also help to keep pest numbers down. Controlling pests in this way, without the use of chemicals, is increasingly popular and should be the first method you consider, especially since encouraging beneficial creatures into a garden introduces greater interest.

BENEFICIAL INSECTS

Getting the terms right ...

• **Beneficial insects:** These are insects that help to control plant-damaging insects • **Biological controls:** See above • **Green gardening:** A term for growing plants without the use of chemicals to control and prevent pests and diseases, as well as for not using artificial chemicals to feed the plants or kill the weeds • **Natural controls:** These encompass the methods for killing plant-attacking insects without chemicals • **Organic gardening:** A popular term for controlling pests and diseases without resorting to the use of chemicals; however, it is a 'hijacked' term as all plants grow organically • **Parasites:** Usually, it is the young stages of parasites that live in or on the body of the pest being attacked • **Predators:** These are insects, as well as other creatures and animals, that roam gardens, killing plant-damaging pests.

Black-kneed capsid bugs

Adult

These bugs lay eggs on apple trees from mid-summer to autumn. They hatch, and the nymphs and adults reduce red spider mite infestations. Nymphs eat 5–40 red spider mites each day, while adults eat 60–70.

Dragonflies

Adult

These attractive insects (including damselflies), as adults, flutter over ponds. The nymphs live in ponds, dykes, marshes, canals and slow-moving streams. In both their nymph and adult stages they will eat other insects.

Green lacewings

Adult

Also known as 'green eyes', they lay batches of greenish eggs on stalks. These hatch, and the larvae eat mainly small aphids, sucking out their body fluids. Each larva eats many hundreds of aphids, as well as mites and leafhoppers.

Powdery lacewings

Larva

Adult

Smaller than green lacewings, they are covered in fine, white powder and resemble greenhouse whiteflies. In orchards, the larvae and adults feed almost entirely on red spider mites and their eggs. Each larva eats 15–35 mites per day.

Ladybirds

Larva

There are many species, with different colours and spots. Both larvae and adults are predators, eating vast numbers of aphids as well as mealy bugs, thrips, mites and scale insects. Each larva of the two-spot ladybird eats 15–20 aphids a day (up to 500 in a three-week larval stage).

Adult

Ground beetles

Adult

These are natural predators, with agile, well-armoured larvae. Both adults and larvae destroy large numbers of small insects, especially at night; they eat large numbers of cabbage root fly eggs, as well as root aphids. The violet ground beetle also attacks slugs.

Larva

Rove beetles

Large family of soil-living beetles, including the devil's coach-horse. Both adult and larvae rove beetles are predators and voraciously consume lettuce root aphids, strawberry aphids and red spider mites. Adult beetles completely devour mites, while larvae suck them.

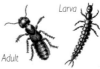
Adult *Larva*

BENEFICIAL INSECTS (CONTINUED)

Ichneumon flies

Mainly parasites of moth and butterfly caterpillars; a few parasitize spiders, lacewings and aphids. Females have long egg-laying parts (ovipositors), enabling them to lay eggs in the bodies of their prey. Eggs hatch and the larvae eat the insect's body, from the inside.

Adult

Braconids

Adult

Parasitical in nature, braconids attack many insects, laying eggs in the caterpillars of a wide range of moths and butterflies. They also attack aphids. The larvae of some braconids, when emerging from their host, build cocoons in a mass.

Chalcids

Large group of mostly parasitical flies that attack butterflies (especially white butterflies), moths (including ermine moths), flies and scale insects, laying eggs in their larvae. Chalcids are more beneficial to gardeners than either ichneumon flies or braconids.

Adult

Hoverflies

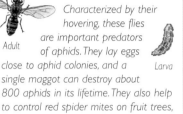

Adult

Characterized by their hovering, these flies are important predators of aphids. They lay eggs close to aphid colonies, and a single maggot can destroy about 800 aphids in its lifetime. They also help to control red spider mites on fruit trees, and lackey moth caterpillars.

Larva

Stiletto flies

Larva

Adult flies have long, tapering abdomens that resemble stilettos. They are predatory; adult flies conceal themselves among low plants or on the soil and prey upon other insects. The slender, predatory larvae resemble wireworms and live in the soil.

Other beneficial insects

Mites: Several mites are pests of gardens, orchards and greenhouse plants, but one of them, *Anystis agilis*, aggressively attacks other mites and insects, especially in orchards.
Brown lacewings: In addition to the green and powdery lacewings (see opposite page), brown lacewings help control aphids, thrips and mites.

RANGE OF OTHER BENEFICIAL CREATURES

• **Centipedes:** Distinguished from millipedes (which damage plants, have a sluggish nature and two pairs of short legs on most body segments) by having one pair of legs on each segment. Centipedes are active creatures and eat slugs, woodlice, mites, leatherjackets, grubs and other insects • **Frogs and toads:** These amphibians have a special liking for slugs and soon keep them under control. Both frogs and toads live in ponds, but are especially useful in a wildlife garden • **Garden spiders:** These are varied but most spin webs that trap insects • **Hedgehogs:** Well-known animal with a voracious appetite for slugs, worms, beetles, earwigs, cutworms and millipedes. Do not disturb them in winter while they are hibernating; check bonfire sites for them before igniting rubbish. Do not provide them with saucers of bread soaked in milk, as this causes diarrhoea in youngsters • **Shrews** and **slow-worms** are also beneficial.

BIOLOGICAL CONTROLS IN GREENHOUSES

• **Aphids:** Use fly larva predators, such as *Aphidoletes aphidimyza* • **Caterpillars:** Use a bacterial disease, such as *Bacillus thuringiensis* • **Mealy bugs:** Encourage the presence of ladybirds • **Red spider mites:** Use the predatory mite *Phytoseiulus persimilis* • **Soft scale insects:** Use the parasitical wasp *Metaphycus helvolus* • **Thrips:** Employ predatory mites (*Amblyseius* spp.) • **Vine weevils:** The larvae can be controlled by a nematode predator (*Heterorhabditis* spp.) • **Whiteflies:** Use the parasitic wasp *Encarsia formosa*.

CROP ROTATION

Growing vegetables continuously on the same piece of soil from one year to another encourages the build-up of pests and diseases. Also, where crops are not rotated the soil becomes depleted of certain plant foods.

Resistant plants

Cultivars of a few plant species have a degree of resistance to some pests and diseases. For example, some butterhead lettuces possess a resistance to lettuce root aphid, while some roses have a resistance to diseases such as black spot, rose rust and powdery mildew.

Companion planting

By using specific plants in association with each other, pest and disease attacks can be diminished. For example: • **Chives** planted between roses help to keep them free of aphids • **Garlic, leeks and onions** grown around beds of carrots help to cloak their distinctive aroma and to confuse carrot fly • **Nasturtiums** especially entice aphids; therefore, plant French marigolds (*Tagetes patula*) nearby as they attract hoverflies that feed on aphids • **Spearmint** and **garlic** help to confuse and deter aphids.

Using pesticides and fungicides

Is there an alternative to chemicals?

Before using any form of pesticide or fungicide, always check that there is no alternative. Dealing with a pest and disease problem is better done by encouraging beneficial and biological methods (see pages 6–7) than by spraying chemicals. Once you have accurately identified the pest or disease (see pages 10–75), and established that there is really no other control available, carefully select the right pesticide or fungicide and follow the instructions below.

Using pesticides and fungicides

Most gardeners resort to the use of pesticides and fungicides only after an attack has been noticed and when plants have been badly damaged. However, this is not the best way to use them, and to be most effective they are best used as a preventative measure, especially when using systemic types; there are both systemic pesticides and systemic fungicides.

What are insecticides?

These are chemicals that are applied either to the plants themselves or to the soil or compost around them. They kill pests by direct contact with them, or by leaving deposits on the plants that they eat. They are ideal for killing insects that chew plants. Other chemicals are absorbed by plants that then become toxic to sap-sucking insects, such as aphids. These types are known as systemic insecticides.

What are pesticides?

Pesticides kill both insects and other pests that are not 'proper' insects (see page 3 for a description and illustration of a typical insect). These non-insect pests embrace mites (which resemble minute spiders and have four pairs of legs), slugs, snails, millipedes and woodlice.

What are fungicides?

These are most effective when sprayed on plants before an attack, rather than when a disease is well established. They act mainly when in contact with the disease. However, systemic fungicides enter a plant's tissue and provide protection from further attacks for several weeks.

GARDEN CHEMICALS: SAFETY FIRST

- Check that the chemical to be used is suitable for combating the problem. Read the label carefully, especially when spraying vegetables, fruits and culinary herbs. Ensure that the correct interval between spraying and harvesting is acknowledged.
- Use clean spraying equipment and containers.
- Do not mix chemicals, unless recommended.
- Wash out sprayers and containers after use; ensure that waste water does not contaminate soil or watercourses.
- Do not spray in bright sunlight, as this may damage plants.
- Wear protective gloves and a face mask.
- Store chemicals in their own containers – do not decant them into other bottles – and keep them out of reach of children.
- If there is a problem, immediately visit a doctor and take along the chemical's container and packaging.

BUYING PESTICIDES, INSECTICIDES AND FUNGICIDES

Knowing which of these to buy to combat problems on specific plants can be confusing, especially as brand names change and periodically chemicals are banned from use as further information about their toxicity and long-term effects become better known. Therefore, the best solution is – through the use of this highly illustrated book which groups plants into types, including border plants, plants for containers, roses, vegetables, soft and tree fruits, culinary herbs, trees and shrubs, lawns, water plants, and greenhouse and houseplants – first to identify the problem. Then check with a reputable garden centre, plant nursery or home hardware store in order to gain advice about the specific chemical that is needed.

IN WHAT FORM SHOULD I BUY THE CHEMICAL?

There are several ways to apply chemicals, and a wide range of them is detailed on the opposite page. For home gardeners, it is more economical to buy only small amounts at one time. Storing them safely can be a problem, as can deterioration if they are kept for an excessively long time.

WHAT ARE HERBICIDES?

Popularly known as weedkillers, they are not related to pesticides, insecticides or fungicides. Instead, they are used to kill plants. Some herbicides destroy all plants and are known as 'total' weedkillers, while others only kill specific weeds, perhaps broad-leaved weeds in lawns, and therefore are known as 'selective' weedkillers. Some are known as 'residual' weedkillers because they are activated when in contact with soil; they can, therefore, be used to spray ground before seeds are sown and plants planted, so that later-germinating weed seedlings are killed.

You should always store weedkillers well away from containers of pesticides, insecticides and fungicides.

HOW TO APPLY CHEMICAL PESTICIDES AND FUNGICIDES

TYPE	USAGE	ADVANTAGES	DISADVANTAGES
Spraying Hand sprays Electric sprayer	Chemicals combined with water to enable them to be spread evenly over plants. Ideal for use on fruit trees and bushes.	Produces a good and quick coverage of foliage (above and below) and stems. But avoid run-off.	Where chemicals are diluted with water, use all of the liquid at the time of application.
Dusting	Chemicals combined with an inert, dust-like carrier for spreading over leaves and stems.	Ready-to-use method and not all of the dust needs to be used at one application. Indoors and outdoors.	Requires a windless day outdoors. Small houseplants can be put in a large plastic bag while being dusted.
Baits and traps Sticky trap Pheromone trap Slug trap Codling moth trap	Baits are ideal for soil-infesting pests, sticky traps for snaring flying and jumping pests, refuge traps for slugs and snails.	Simple and easy to use and do not contaminate gardens or greenhouses with chemicals.	Need regular checking to remove snared or trapped insects or other pests.
Insecticidal sticks	Ideal for indoor, green-house and conservatory plants. Easily and quickly inserted in compost.	Can be stored while awaiting use; roots absorb chemicals from the sticks, which make plants toxic to insects.	Have to be replaced regularly, as and when the chemicals are used (check frequency with the instructions).
Aerosols and fumigants Aerosol Fumigant	Greenhouses only. Fumigants are smoke-based, while aerosols produce a mist of fine liquid droplets.	Quick and easy to use, encapsulating all plants in an insecticide.	Fumigants need a temperature of at least 18°C (64°F); leave green-houses closed overnight.
Seed dressings	Insecticides and fungicides combined with seeds. Ideal where the risk from pests and diseases is known and expected.	Acts as a preventative measure before the damage is noticed. Ideal for combating flea beetles.	Treated seeds are more expensive than non-treated ones.
Grease bands and slippery tapes Grease band Slippery tape	Grease bands are wrapped around trunks of fruit trees in early autumn to prevent wingless adult females of the winter moth climbing the trunk. Slippery tapes around pots and tubs prevent slugs and snails reaching plants.	Non-chemical and inexpensive ways to prevent pest damage, both in orchards and on patios.	Remove grease bands in spring. Regularly check slippery tapes to ensure they are effective.

CHEMICALS INDOORS

As well as the same safety considerations when using chemicals in gardens, remember:

- Avoid spraying if children and household pets are in the same room; fish and birds are especially susceptible to chemical sprays.
- Never allow children to touch, or animals to lick or chew, plants that have been sprayed.
- Take care not to spray curtains (drapes) and other fabrics.

SAFETY FOR PETS AND WILDLIFE

- Plant-eating pets, such as guinea pigs and rabbits, must be kept off grass treated with herbicides (weedkillers) until after it has received its first cut.
- Avoid contaminating bird baths and fish ponds, as well as animals' water bowls left outside in summer.
- When spraying outdoors, leave it until late in the day, when bees and beneficial insects are not flying.
- When using slug pellets, ensure that wild animals cannot reach them.

SAFE DISPOSAL OF GARDEN CHEMICALS

Do not just tip unused chemicals down a drain or empty into a watercourse. Instead, contact your local waste disposal authority and ask for advice. Do not remove labels from bottles and packages, as they may give the waste disposal authority an indication of their safe disposal.

Border flowers and bedding plants

What are the main pests?

The range is wide, from pests that chew leaves and flowers to ones that suck sap, causing puckering, yellowing and distortion. Most sap-sucking types, such as aphids, also transmit viruses from plant to plant. Some insects attack specific plants, such as chrysanthemum eelworms on chrysanthemums, whereas others infest many different border and bedding plants. A few pests, such as flea beetles, attack specific ornamental plants as well as cabbages.

PESTS OF FLOWERS, STEMS AND LEAVES

Caterpillars

These chew soft leaves and stems, making them unsightly. Pick off and destroy caterpillars as soon as you spot them. Additionally, spray plants with an insecticide at 10-day intervals. Pull up and burn plants in autumn.

Leafhoppers

These small, pale yellow insects pierce undersides of leaves, creating light mottling on the upper surface. When disturbed, they jump and fly away. They infest many plants, including roses and pelargoniums. Spray with an insecticide.

Pea and bean weevils

These pests mainly attack peas and beans, but also sweet peas. Leaf edges are chewed, sometimes producing 'U-shaped' notching. The growing points of plants are often chewed in spring. Use an insecticide; also dig the soil in winter and burn all rubbish.

Snails

These pests chew and tear leaves, stems and flowers, as well as roots, tubers, bulbs and corms. They hide during the day and come out at night. Use baits and traps; see pages 6–7 for non-chemical controls.

Slugs

They have similar natures and appetites to snails, but usually inflict more damage. Use baits and traps; see pages 6–7 for non-chemical controls.

Flea beetles

They usually chew the leaves of cabbages, turnips and other brassicas, as well as wallflowers, sweet alyssum and iberis, especially in late spring and early summer and when the weather is dry. Use an insecticide; additionally, in autumn remove and burn rubbish and weeds.

Woodlice

They mainly come out at night and chew leaves, stems, flowers and roots, and are often prevalent in areas near old buildings and greenhouses. Dust with an insecticide and remove rubbish and other hiding places. They are also known as 'pillbugs', 'slaters' and 'sowbugs'.

Froghoppers

Young froghoppers produce froth known as cuckoo spit, usually on stems and near sideshoots, especially on plants such as roses, annual chrysanthemums, phlox, coreopsis and campanulas. Froghoppers suck sap and distort growth. Although insecticides can be used, the froth is easily removed by a jet of water.

Chrysanthemum eelworms

These are nematodes (microscopic eel-worms that burrow within leaves) causing areas of chrysanthemum leaves to become blackened. Other herbaceous plants are also susceptible. Severe infestations kill plants. The best control is to buy healthy plants.

Leaf miners

The larvae of some flies and moths bore into leaves, creating narrow, meandering tunnels that sometimes become blotches. Chrysanthemums are frequently attacked. Spraying with an insecticide is not usually necessary; just pick off infected leaves.

Black bean aphids

A type of aphid that infests many border plants including nasturtiums, dahlias and poppies. They cluster on stems, leaves and flowers, sucking the sap and distorting growth. Spray with a systemic insecticide.

Thrips

These are often a pest in greenhouses as well as borders, puncturing leaves and flowers and causing silvery mottling of plants including gladioli, sweet peas and honeysuckles. Spray with an insecticide as soon as damage becomes obvious, and keep plants well watered.

Capsid bugs

The tarnished plant bug or bishop bug attacks the flowers of many kinds of bedding and border plants, such as chrysanthemums and dahlias. Both adults and nymphs pierce tissue and suck sap. Leaves and flowers become deformed. Spray with an insecticide.

Birds

Birds peck and damage blossom, young shoots and fruits. In borders, leaves and buds of chrysanthemums and carnations are often damaged. Sparrows especially have a likening for polyanthus and other primulas, as well as crocuses. Use bird scarers.

Aphids

Also known as greenfly and aphis, these pests infest many kinds of border and bedding plants, clustering on stems, leaves, buds and flowers, sucking sap and distorting growth. Spray with a systemic insecticide.

Earwigs

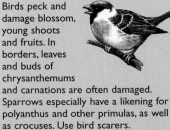

Widely seen attacking border plants, especially chrysanthemums and dahlias. They hide during the day and attack at night, chewing and ripping petals and soft stems and leaves. Pick them off or use an insecticide. Also, trap them in straw-packed pots inverted on canes.

DISEASES OF FLOWERS, STEMS AND LEAVES
OF BORDER FLOWERS AND BEDDING PLANTS

Downy mildew

White, fluffy or mealy fungal growth on undersides of leaves; upper sides blotched either dull green or yellow. Growth is stunted, with older leaves unsightly. It is encouraged by congested and humid conditions. Spray with a fungicide, although control is difficult.

Grey mould (Botrytis)

Soft-leaved plants are especially vulnerable, with a grey fungal growth on foliage, stems and flowers. Areas discolour and deteriorate. Damp conditions encourage spread, especially through damaged leaves and stems. Avoid congestion and spray with a systemic fungicide.

Tulip breaking virus

Sometimes known as 'colour breaking', it affects tulips and, to a lesser extent, lilies. Flowers become streaked in different colours. Leaves may also be affected. The virus is spread by sap-sucking pests such as aphids, so spray to control them and always buy virus-free bulbs.

Leaf spot

Several fungi and bacteria cause spots on leaves. Most affect specific plants and are unlikely to spread to other species. Remove infected leaves, use a fungicide and feed poorly growing plants. In autumn, remove and burn infected leaves to prevent the disease overwintering.

Sooty mould

Black, soot-like, fungal mould, initially lightly covering leaves but later resulting in total coverage. Also infests buds, shoots and flowers. It grows on honeydew, excreted by insects such as aphids. Spray to control sap-sucking pests and use a damp, soft cloth to wipe off early signs of infection.

Tulip fire

Serious fungal disease of tulips. Symptoms include deformed shoots and leaves; scorched tips of young leaves; small, sunken, grey spots on leaves; unopened flower buds; brown spots on flowers. Burn infected plants and buy clean bulbs each year. Do not grow bulbs in affected soil for four years.

Powdery mildew

Fungi create a white, powdery coating of spores on leaves (both sides) and stems; sometimes coats flowers and fruits. Infected border plants include delphiniums, chrysanthemums and begonias. Encouraged by dampness, dryness at roots and poor air circulation. Water soil and use a systemic fungicide.

Petal blight

Fungal disease that infects anemones, chrysanthemums and dahlias. The fungus causes browning petals and, later, decay and withering. Excess humidity and still air create ideal conditions for its spread. Burn infected flowers and spray with a fungicide.

Wilt (Verticillium)

Fungus that infects many plants, including herbaceous perennials, causing brown or black discoloration on leaves and stems. Later, plants wilt. It mainly enters plants through damaged stems and leaves. Dig up and burn infected herbaceous plants.

Rust

Many different rusts, each with a complex life cycle. Affects many plants, including pelargoniums, chrysanthemums and carnations. First noticed as raised, brown or black areas on foliage. Spray with a rust fungicide. Seriously infected plants are best discarded and burned.

Damping off

Serious fungal disease. Seedlings in seed-trays in greenhouses collapse, especially if sown thickly and in badly drained and compacted compost, without good ventilation and in high temperatures. May also attack seedlings outdoors. Use clean compost and water the compost with a fungicide.

ROOT AND BULB PROBLEMS
OF BORDER FLOWERS AND BEDDING PLANTS

Leatherjackets

Fat, legless, grey-brown grubs, the larvae of the cranefly (daddy-longlegs). Adults lay eggs in the soil; they hatch and grubs feed on roots. Prevalent on soil newly cultivated from pasture land. Thoroughly cultivate land in winter in preparation for ornamental plants. Dust with an insecticide.

Narcissus fly

Larvae of the large narcissus fly tunnel into daffodils, irises, lilies and hyacinths, eventually causing decay, especially around their necks. Burn infected bulbs and buy only sound bulbs from a reliable source. Hoe around bulbs to disturb the soil.

Clubroot

Also known as 'finger-and-toe', this fungal disease attacks members of the cabbage family (including wallflowers). Roots become swollen, gnarled and knotted, with plants stunted. It is encouraged by slightly acid and badly drained soil. Do not replant on the same land for four years; dip roots in a fungicidal suspension before planting.

Cutworms

Caterpillars of several moths (turnip moth, heart and dart moth, and large yellow underwing moth). They gnaw stems at ground level, causing plants to wilt, and mainly feed at night. Pick off and burn caterpillars and regularly hoe soil surface. Also use an insecticide.

Millipedes

Millipedes damage plants, feeding on roots, bulbs, tubers and corms, often after damage initially caused by slugs and wireworms. In autumn, burn all rubbish and, when preparing a new bed in winter, deeply cultivate the soil. Dust the soil with a pesticide.

Fungus gnats

Also known as 'mushroom flies'. Small, gnat-like, black flies (themselves harmless) lay eggs in compost and result in white, legless larvae that normally feed on organic material in compost, but occasionally attack roots of seedlings. Soft-stemmed plants are also at risk. Drench the soil in an insecticide.

Cockchafer grubs

Also known as 'May bugs' or 'June bugs', their larvae live in soil and feed on roots of herbaceous and other plants, causing wilting and death. They are prevalent in land newly converted from grassland. Dig the soil in winter before converting to flower beds. Dust soil with an insecticide.

Rhizome rot

Soil-infesting bacterial soft rot that infests rhizomatous irises, especially during wet seasons. It enters through wounds and is encouraged by poor soil drainage. Burn badly infected rhizomes, dust cuts with a fungicide and control pests such as slugs and wireworms.

Slugs

Well-known pests that hide during the day and come out at night. They are encouraged by damp conditions, eating roots, bulbs, tubers and corms. Use baits and traps; see pages 6–7 for non-chemical controls.

Snails

Similar appetites and natures to slugs. They hide in rubbish and under stones and are especially active at night, during periods of damp and mild weather; they soon devastate plants. Use baits and traps; see pages 6–7 for non-chemical controls.

Stem and bulb eelworms

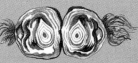

Serious pest of daffodils, hyacinths and tulips. Microscopic eelworms enter leaves and stems and, in daffodils and hyacinths, cause twisting and distortion. Bulbs become soft and rotten. Pull up and burn infected bulbs and do not plant susceptible plants in the same area for three years. Always buy clean bulbs.

Vine weevils

Both adult beetles and their fat, legless, creamy-white larvae infest garden and greenhouse plants. In rock gardens, the larvae can be devastating, eating roots and tunnelling into bulbs, corms and tubers. Trap adult weevils in spring in rolled pieces of sacking or corrugated paper.

Wireworms

Distinctive larvae of the click beetle or 'skip-jack'; chew roots, stems, corms and tubers. Prevalent on newly cultivated land. Dust soil with a pesticide. Trapping is possible by shallowly burying cut carrots or potatoes and removing them when contaminated with wireworms.

Swift moths

Several types of these moths and their larvae feed on herbaceous plants and tunnel into daffodil bulbs, gladiolus corms, iris rhizomes and dahlia tubers. They are most prevalent on newly cultivated land. Dust soil with an insecticide.

Ornamental trees and shrubs

Are they seriously attacked?

Ornamental trees and shrubs are relatively free from pests, and even when attacked are usually able to survive, although parts of them may, briefly, lose their visual appeal. Aphids attack soft stems, leaves and flowers; the holly leaf miner burrows into tough holly leaves; and scale insects tightly adhere to branches of shrubs such as *Cotoneaster*. Here are a few pests you may encounter, together with suggested treatments.

Rhododendron whitefly

Infest species and hybrid rhododendrons, especially in mild areas. The small, white, mealy-covered, winged, moth-like insects appear in early and mid-summer, causing yellowish mottling on leaves. Honeydew (later, sooty mould) often appears on leaves. Spray with a contact or systemic insecticide.

Holly leaf miners

In late spring, small, black flies lay eggs on leaves. These hatch and the larvae burrow into leaves, creating mines and, eventually, blisters. Difficult to control; pick off infected leaves and spray with a systemic insecticide in early summer.

Woolly aphids (American blight)

Infest many ornamental trees and shrubs, including *Cotoneaster, Malus, Pyracantha* and *Pyrus*. Twigs and branches become covered with a white, wool-like wax. Brush colonies with an insecticide; or spray them with a contact or systemic insecticide.

Aphids (greenfly)

Many aphids infest soft shoots and leaves of shrubs and trees, especially during early summer. They form clusters and suck sap, causing distortion and, sometimes, puckering. Aphids also excrete honeydew, which encourages the presence of sooty mould. Spray with a systemic insecticide.

Leaf-eating weevils

Destructive pests on ornamental trees and shrubs, feeding on leaves by clinically cutting out segments. As soon as adult weevils or their damage is seen, spray with a contact insecticide.

Lackey moths

Common pest of ornamental apples, pears and cherries, as well as hawthorn, roses and willow. In late summer, moths lay eggs; these hatch in spring. Plants are sometimes defoliated. Distinctively, the moths create silken 'tents' in which they pupate. Cut out and burn the 'tents', and spray with a contact insecticide.

Leopard moths

As well as infesting fruit trees, these colourful moths attack ornamental trees and shrubs, such as lilac and rhododendron. Caterpillars are wood borers and the first sign of attack is wilting leaves. Small entry holes are surrounded by 'frass'. Cut back infections to sound wood.

Winter moths

Include several leaf-eating pests of fruit trees and bushes; also, ornamental flowering cherries and pears. Caterpillars, which appear in spring, have a characteristic 'looping' nature and sometimes loosely spin leaves together. They eat holes in leaves. Apply a winter-wash. Also use grease bands (see pages 9 and 77).

Tortrix or leaf-rolling moths

Several ornamental trees and shrubs are attacked, including *Cornus* (Dogwood), hawthorns, hollies, rhododendrons, and ornamental pear and cherry trees. Distinctively, moths roll leaves and tie their edges together. Larvae often hang down on a silken thread. Use a forceful insecticidal spray.

Scale insects

Several scale insects attack ornamental trees and shrubs, including *Aucuba, Azara, Camellia, Carpenteria, Ceanothus, Cotoneaster, Escallonia, Pyrus* and *Taxus* (Yew). Infestations are first seen when plants become sticky and covered with waxy, brown, white or yellow scales. Spray with a systemic insecticide. Also spray with a winter-wash.

Mussel scale

Plants in containers

What are the main pests?

Most plants grown in hanging-baskets are, at some stage, likely to be infested by airborne pests such as aphids (greenfly and blackfly) as well as whitefly. Plants that are growing in pots, tubs and troughs displayed at ground level are at risk from crawling and creeping pests such as slugs, snails, woodlice and earwigs, which can soon decimate leaves, stems and flowers, rendering an attractive display quite unsightly.

PESTS AND DISEASES OF FLOWERS, STEMS AND LEAVES IN CONTAINERS OUTDOORS AND IN LOBBIES

Rust

Several types of rust infest plants grown in containers. Some rusts spend all their lives on one plant, while others have several hosts. Pick off and burn infected leaves, remove seriously infected plants, increase ventilation around plants and use a rust fungicide.

Aphids (greenfly)

Infest many soft leaves and stems, as well as flowers, sucking sap, transmitting viruses and causing debilitation. Use a systemic insecticide early in the season, before an infestation reaches epidemic proportions. Later sprayings are also usually necessary.

Slugs

Like snails, these are nature's stealth pests, hiding during the day and coming out at night to decimate plants. They often climb containers, as well as walls, to get at the plants. Pick off and burn them, and use baits and traps. Encircle containers with slippery tapes, over which they cannot pass.

Cuckoo spit

Froth-like foam protects nymphs of the common froghopper, sometimes known as 'spittle bug', from birds and other predators. Both adult insects and nymphs suck sap. Use jets of water to remove the spittle and a systemic insecticide to kill the insects.

Earwigs

Pernicious pests, hiding during the day and chewing and tearing leaves, flowers and soft stems at night. Pick off and burn them. Also remove rubbish from around plants and spray with a pesticide. Thoroughly clean each container in autumn.

Snails

They have habits similar to slugs, hiding under debris and in crevices during the day and eating plants at night. Pick off and burn them, and use baits and traps. Also encircle containers with wide, slippery tapes to prevent access to the plants.

Caterpillars

These have voracious appetites and soon decimate soft leaves, stems and flowers. Pick off caterpillars and burn them. Spray plants with a contact insecticide at ten-day intervals. At the end of summer, pull up and burn infested plants.

Woodlice

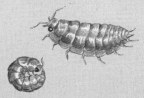

They climb walls and infest wall-baskets and windowboxes, as well as plants in pots, tubs and growing-bags on a patio floor. They mainly come out of hiding at night, chewing leaves, stems, flowers and roots. Dust with a pesticide and burn all rubbish in autumn. Also known as 'pillbugs', 'slaters' and 'sowbugs'.

Whitefly

These small, moth-like insects flutter from one plant to another, sucking sap and causing mottling and debilitation. They excrete honeydew, which encourages the presence of sooty mould. Spray plants with a systemic insecticide.

Vine weevils

Both adults and larvae are destructive; larvae chew roots, causing plants to wilt, while adults eat leaves. Chewed foliage is soon evident, but not the damage to roots. Pick off and burn beetles. Use a systemic insecticide on the foliage, and drench the compost.

PESTS AND DISEASES OF FLOWERS, STEMS AND LEAVES
IN CONTAINERS OUTDOORS AND IN LOBBIES (CONTINUED)

Thrips

Sometimes known as 'thunder flies', these minute, elongated insects pierce leaves and flowers, sucking sap and often causing silvery mottling. Severe infestation dramatically affects plants. Spray with a systemic insecticide as soon as damage is seen, and keep the compost moist.

Red spider mites

Sometimes seen on plants in warm lobbies. These eight-legged, minute, spider-like creatures infest undersides of leaves, causing bronzing on upper surfaces. They sometimes form webbing. Mist-spray plants daily, pick off infected leaves and use a systemic acaricide.

Cyclamen mites

Often seen on cyclamen, impatiens and pelargoniums indoors. They infest undersides of leaves, causing bronzing on upper surfaces; flowers become distorted and stunted. Burn infected leaves and use an acaricide.

Mealy bugs

Resemble small, white, mealy woodlice; sometimes found in warm lobbies on a wide range of plants. They especially crowd around junctions of leaves and stems, and on shoots and leaves. Wipe off with a cotton bud dipped in methylated spirits, or use a systemic insecticide.

Grey mould (Botrytis)

Fluffy, grey mould on soft stems, leaves, buds and flowers, encouraged by high humidity; although normally a diseases of greenhouses and houseplants, it can also be seen in warm, badly ventilated and damp lobbies. Cut off and burn infected parts, improve ventilation, avoid having wet compost and use a systemic fungicide.

Leaf spot

Both fungi and bacteria cause spots on leaves of plants, mostly in greenhouses but sometimes in humid and badly ventilated lobbies. Remove and burn infected leaves, keep the foliage dry and spray with a systemic fungicide. Feed plants with a balanced fertilizer.

Powdery mildew

Fungi that produces a white, powdery covering of spores on leaves (both sides) and stems. It is encouraged by excessive humidity and lack of ventilation. Remove and burn badly infected leaves and spray with a systemic fungicide.

Viruses

Many different viruses, causing distortion and stunted growth. Leaves assume yellow and pale green areas between their veins. Viruses are spread by sap-sucking insects, such as aphids, and contamination through infected plants when being vegetatively increased. Burn badly infected plants and regularly spray against aphids and other sap-sucking insects.

Roses

Are they all susceptible?

Most roses, whether they are growing in beds, scaling walls or clinging to pillars and tripods, are susceptible to a variety of pests and diseases. However, well-grown roses are less likely to be serious damaged than those that are weak and badly nourished. Good garden hygiene, including regular pruning, removing fallen leaves and clearing away weeds, helps to deter pests and diseases from attacking these popular flowering plants.

PESTS OF ROSES

Aphids (greenfly)

Aphids often infest roses, clustering around flower buds and on stems and young shoots. They suck sap and are especially present in spring and early summer, when young, new shoots appear. Growth is distorted and debilitated, while the aphids excrete honeydew, which encourages the presence of ants and sooty mould. Spray with a systemic insecticide. Do not wait until an infestation reaches epidemic proportions before using an insecticide.

Birds

Birds occasionally tear at buds, shoots, leaves and flowers, often just in spite and because there are no other plants for them to attack. They are at their most damaging when pecking and tearing young buds and can soon destroy the prospect of flowers for a complete season. Deterring them is a difficult task (see page 30), because legally they must not be harmed.

Caterpillars

Several caterpillars chew leaves of roses, causing irregularly shaped holes. These include the larvae of the buff-tip moth, the vapourer moth, the winter moth and the yellow-tail moth. If the infestation is only small, pick off and burn them. Alternatively, spray with a contact insecticide.

These pests often hide among clusters of leaves and initially are difficult to see until they have done a great deal of damage. Therefore, regularly check among the leaves.

Cockchafer beetles

Several types; adult beetles chew leaves and flowers, while fat, white, curved larvae damage roots. Adult beetles are easily picked off and burned; they are mainly seen in late spring and early summer. If infestations are severe, spray with a contact insecticide. The larvae, however, can cause more damage through chewing roots. Before planting roses, dig the soil to expose the larvae and, in spring, rake an insecticide into the soil.

Cockchafer

Garden chafer

Capsid bugs

Nymphs

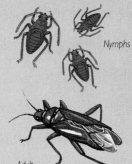

Adult

Apart from rasping and tearing leaves, and causing small brown spots on young leaves, the capsids chew buds and inject toxic saliva that kills plant tissue. The bright green capsids move quickly when disturbed. Spray plants with a contact or systemic insecticide as soon as damage is noticed.

Cuckoo spit

Froth-like foam protects nymphs of the common froghopper, sometimes known as 'spittle bug', from birds and other predators. Both adult insects and nymphs suck sap. Use jets of water to remove the spittle and a systemic insecticide to kill the insects.

Lackey moths

Common pest on fruit and ornamental trees, as well as roses. The caterpillars live in colonies, chewing irregularly shaped holes in leaves, and can cause complete defoliation. They create silken 'tents', in which they pupate. Cut off the 'tents' and spray with a contact or systemic insecticide. The 'tents' make the problem easy to identify; but regularly check among the foliage for caterpillar colonies.

PESTS OF ROSES (CONTINUED)

Leaf miners

Leaves are mined by larvae burrowing into them, creating ribbon-like tunnels. Sometimes, the tunnels merge and form blisters. Often, the grub can be seen within a tunnel. Pick off and burn badly affected leaves and use a contact insecticide. If the infestation is small, just crush the larva within the leaf. Systemic insecticides can be used to prevent further incursions.

Leaf-rolling rose sawfly

The edges of leaflets become tightly rolled inwards along their lengths, causing them to shrivel and, eventually, to die. If unrolled, a greenish-grey larva is revealed and can be removed and killed. Some varieties are especially susceptible, including 'Peace', 'The Queen Elizabeth' and 'New Dawn'. Shallowly hoe around roses in winter and early spring, pick off and burn seriously infected leaves and spray with a contact insecticide in late spring and early summer.

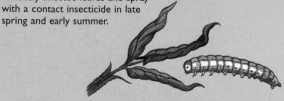

Rose leafhoppers

Upper sides of leaves assume pale, mottled patches and, in severe infestations, leaves fall off, especially if the weather is dry. Climbing roses against walls are especially at risk. Eggs laid in autumn overwinter and produce a brood in late spring and early summer. A second generation sometimes appears in late summer and early autumn. Spray with a systemic insecticide during late spring or early summer, and again later if an infestation is noticed.

Red spider mites

Minute, eight-legged and spider-like, they are mainly found on the undersides of leaves, causing fine, light speckling on the upper surface. Later, these become bronze and patch-like, with fine webbing on the undersides. Infestations are worse during hot, dry weather. Regularly mist-spray the foliage with clean water and spray with a systemic insecticide as soon as damage is noticed.

Scurfy scale

Sometimes known as 'rose scale', the small, round and flat, white scales appear in dense clusters, especially on old and neglected stems. They are unsightly and plants become weakened. If the infestation is localized, cut out infested shoots or paint with methylated spirits. Severe infestations need to be sprayed with a systemic insecticide.

Rose slugworm sawfly

Sometimes known as 'rose slugworm' or 'rose skeletonizer', the larvae feed on the undersides of leaves, skeletonizing areas between the veins. These areas turn brown, assume a shrivelled nature and become unsightly. The slug-like larvae are brownish- or greenish-yellow. Pick them off and spray with a contact insecticide. Also, in winter and early spring, shallowly hoe under roses to disturb and expose overwintering larvae.

Tortrix moths

Sometimes known as 'rose maggots', the distinctive, brown or green caterpillars spin together the edges of leaves, enclosing them and creating protection for themselves. The larvae often hang down on a silken thread. If the infestation is slight, pick off and burn the affected leaves; but usually it is necessary to use a contact spray, applied forcefully so that it penetrates inside the curled leaves.

DISEASES AND PHYSIOLOGICAL DISORDERS OF ROSES

Blindness

Physiological disorder in which growing points cease to develop or flower buds turn brown and wither. Caused by many factors, including dryness around the plant's roots, waterlogged soil, frost and insufficient feeding. Some varieties, such as 'Peace', are prone to this problem. Cut blind shoots back to at least half their lengths, to just above a healthy bud. This will encourage the remaining part of the old stem to form a young shoot that will produce a flower.

Balling

Physiological disorder in which flower buds fail to open and turn brown. The flower bud does not collapse. Plants with large, thin flower petals or growing in shaded positions are most susceptible, especially during wet weather. Feed plants with a balanced fertilizer.

Crown gall

Unsightly problem, caused by a gall-initiating disease that produces large, wart-like, distorted growths close to the bases of stems. Infection initially comes from bacteria splashed on low, damaged stems. Use clean secateurs to cut out each gall to the base of its stem. Burn infected stems to prevent further spread – do not just leave them on the ground.

Rose black spot

Well-known rose disease, first appearing in early summer and resulting in spreading, dark brown or black spots with irregular yellow fringes. Infected leaves usually fall off. Severe infestations damage buds as well as stems. Difficult to control and preventative measures involve burning all infected leaves and repeated sprays of a fungicide. Also feed with a balanced fertilizer.

Black spot-resistant roses include 'Alexander', 'Blessings', 'King's Ransom', 'Marlena', 'Peace', 'Super Star', 'Sutter's Gold' and 'The Queen Elizabeth'.

Rose canker

Appears as an open, sunken, brown wound close to the base of a stem. Edges are often swollen and the bark cracked. If the canker spreads, it may eventually encircle a stem and cause death. Canker is caused by pest or disease damage, as well as by being clipped with a hoe. Cut off and burn affected shoots and ensure that the plant is given a balanced fertilizer.

Dieback

Shoots die back, sometimes followed by branches. It can be caused by fungal diseases entering through shoots that have been damaged by a pest, by mechanical means or by frost. Cut off damaged shoots to buds below the infection, feed with a balance fertilizer (but not late in the year) and spray to control pests.

Rose rust

Well-known and sometimes fatal rose disease, with small, orange-yellow spots appearing on the undersides of leaves during early and mid-summer. These spots gradually change to dark brown or black. Pick off and burn infected leaves; also, burn prunings. Cold weather and a shortage of potash exacerbates the problem. Spray with a rust fungicide.

Rose powdery mildew

Sometimes known as 'rose mildew', this pernicious and widespread disease results in white, powdery mould on leaves and buds. Leaves may turn yellow, wither and drop off, while buds fail to open. Congested conditions, hot days followed by cold nights, dryness at their roots and imbalanced feeding encourages powdery mildew. Choose mildew-resistant varieties and spray with a fungicide.

ROOT PROBLEMS OF ROSES

Ants

These are pernicious and widespread, disturbing and loosening soil around roots, especially where the soil is light. Plants then wilt and, occasionally, die. Dust with an antkiller.

Chafer grubs

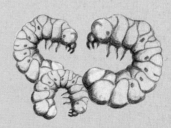

Several types of chafer grubs graze on roots, seriously weakening plants. Pick off and burn adult beetles. Before planting roses, dig the soil deeply in early winter to expose the larvae to birds and frost. If they are present in established rose beds, dust the soil with an insecticide. See page 23 for the adult beetles.

Water-garden plants

Can chemicals be used?

Pesticides and fungicides cannot be used on plants that are growing in ponds, because fish and other occupants, as well as beneficial insects and wildlife, would be killed. Often, insect pests can be washed off leaves for fish to eat, or drowned by temporarily weighing down leaves beneath the water's surface. As a preventative measure, buy pest- and disease-free plants from reputable sources. There are many water-garden specialist nurseries and expert garden centres.

Brown China mark moths

Moths lay eggs on waterlily pads in late summer, resulting in tapering, cream-coloured, worm-like, 2.5 cm (1 in)  long, caterpillars with dark heads and a dark brown line along their backs. They cut off pieces of leaves (which they use as protective 'cases'), leaving foliage that starts to decay. Pick off the floating 'cases' and submerge the lily pads.

Leaf-mining midges

Destructive pests, with eggs laid on a wide range of aquatic plants, including waterlilies. The eggs hatch and produce small, transparent, thin  larvae that tunnel into leaves, eating soft tissue and soon skeletonizing plants. Cut off badly infested leaves or submerge them to enable fish to find the larvae.

Waterlily aphids

Dark green or brown aphids crowd on leaves and flower buds of waterlilies and other aquatic plants, causing distortion and deterioration. Immediately the aphids are noticed, either submerge the leaves for the fish to eat them, or wash off with a jet of water.

Waterlily beetles

Destructive, with both brown beetles (with lighter brown markings) and fat, yellow-bellied, brown-black larvae eating holes in the upper surfaces of leaves. Either submerge the leaves for a day or so, or use a forceful jet of water to knock them off so that fish can eat them.

Iris sawfly

Pest of waterside irises, such as *Iris laevigata* and *Iris pseudacorus*; large pieces along the edges of leaves are eaten. Dull, bluish-grey larvae hatch from eggs laid in early summer and feed mainly in mid-summer. Pick off and burn the larvae, remove badly infested leaves or use a jet of water to dislodge them into the water.

Bloodworms

About 18 mm (¾ in) long, these are the larvae of non-biting midges and are found in the top 5 cm (2 in) of soil in the bases of ponds. They are red and mainly feed on dead plant and animal material, but occasionally on roots of waterlilies and other aquatic plants. No control is necessary as they are soon eaten by fish.

Snails

Most ponds have snails; usually, their numbers are in balance with their dietary habits in eating the waste of fish and algae. Sometimes, however, there are too many of them and they start to attack healthy plants. If this happens, put a cabbage leaf in the pond; they collect on it and later it can be removed.

Caddis fly

If fish are present, the caddis fly larvae have a short life and this pest therefore causes few problems in ponds. The adult flies visit ponds in the evenings, laying eggs in or near water. The larvae are mostly aquatic and make homes in bits of plants. However, they feed on these plants, damaging roots, flower buds and leaves. The best control is to stock the pond with fish.

DISEASES OF WATERLILIES

Waterlily leaf spot

An occasional disease, initially seen as rounded spots but later enlarging and with an irregular outline; they change from reddish- to grey-brown and finally black. Warm, damp weather encourages its presence. Pull off infected leaves — do not spray.

Waterlily crown rot

Serious disease of waterlilies; leaves become yellow and break away from the crown, which becomes black, decayed and with a putrid smell. There is no cure; once it is established, the only solution is to empty the pond, clean it thoroughly and plant waterlilies bought from a reputable source.

Rock-garden plants

Are there many problems?

Pests and diseases in rock gardens are varied, from birds pecking at flowers to moles, mice and cats. Yet they are all controllable, and should not turn into major problems. Poorly drained soil encourages plant roots to decay, while slugs and snails are ever present and especially damaging at night and during spells of damp weather. Aphids (greenfly) are often tempted by young, soft shoots and flowers, especially in spring and early summer.

PESTS OF FLOWERS, LEAVES, STEMS, ROOTS, BULBS AND CORMS

Birds

Birds, including sparrows, bullfinches and blackbirds, are tempted by flowers and in spring are especially attracted to crocuses and primulas. They also disturb young plants in their hunt for grubs. Black strings tied over plants sometimes deter birds, but the birds must not be harmed. Silver-foil strips tied to bamboo canes also deter them.

Aphids

Both greenfly and blackfly infest young leaves, shoots and flowers, especially in early summer. They suck sap, causing distortion, and excrete honeydew, which attracts ants and encourages the presence of sooty mould (black and unsightly). Use a systemic insecticide, and keep plants watered during dry weather.

Caterpillars

Angle shades moth

In early summer, many leaf-eating caterpillars infest rock-garden plants. They chew leaves, soon creating unsightly holes. Keep a check on plants and pick off and burn the caterpillars. Also spray with a contact or systemic insecticide.

Cats

Cats are a problem on light soils and where there is a thin mulch of pea-shingle. They delight in scratching the surface, soon damaging new plants and bulbs. Cats are less likely to scratch thick coverings of larger stones. Dusting the surface with pepper also deters them.

Slugs

Slugs soon decimate leaves and shoots; they hide during the day and devour plants at night, especially during damp weather. Clear away rubbish and hiding areas and use slug pellets. Traps and broken eggshells around plants also help to deter them.

Snails

These affect plants in the same way as slugs. At night – as well as during the early morning – pick off and burn them. Also use baits, traps and broken eggshells to deter them. Usually, snails are less of a problem than slugs.

Cutworms

Fat, grey-brown or green caterpillars, the larvae of various moths. They eat at night, chewing leaves and appearing to sever stems at soil level. Sometimes they are present in newly constructed rock gardens. Mulches of grit or pea-shingle deter them. Also remove all weeds and dust soil with an insecticide.

Auricula root aphids

Feed on roots of auriculas and certain other primulas. Foliage turns yellow and wilts and, eventually, plants die. The greenish-white, mealy and wax-covered aphids cluster on roots and the bases of stems. Drench the soil around the roots with a systemic insecticide.

Moles

Occasionally, moles are a problem, resulting in tunnels, mounds of soil and root disturbance. Whatever the solution to a mole problem, remember that the animal must not be harmed. Blocking tunnels (not always successful) and planting 'repellent' plants, such as *Euphorbia lathyris* (Caper Spurge, Myrtle Spurge, Mole Plant), close by deters them.

Ants

Pernicious and determined pests that loosen soil around plants, especially when it is light. Plants then wilt and, occasionally, die. Dust with an antkiller.

Mice

In seasons when food is scarce, mice dig down and around plants to reach bulbs and corms. The wood mouse is usually the culprit; they do not hibernate and remain active throughout winter. Cover 'at-risk' areas with 1 cm (⅜ in) wire-mesh, and use humane traps.

Vine weevils

Both adults and larvae are destructive; the larvae chew roots, while adults eat leaves. They can soon destroy roots, causing plants to wilt. Pick off and burn the adults, and use a contact or systemic insecticide on the foliage; also drench the compost.

Grey mould (Botrytis)

Fluffy, grey mould appears on soft stems, leaves, buds and flowers. It is encouraged by wet seasons. Pick off and burn infected flowers and leaves. Spray plants with a systemic fungicide at the earliest opportunity. Plants that are severely damaged will have to be pulled up and burned.

Lawns

Grass is pretty resilient and at first glance often appears to be free of pests, diseases or cultural problems. However, a detailed inspection often reveals bare or brown areas, or perhaps mounds of sticky soil produced by worms. There also may be patches of a fungal-based disease. The attentions of dogs and children also impose wear on grass, which can cloak the intrusions of pests and diseases. Regularly inspect the lawn throughout the year.

PESTS OF LAWNS

Dogs

Dogs scratch and tear up lawns, while bitches recurringly urinate on chosen areas, causing brown then yellow patches. Training puppies to use out-of-the-way places in gardens as lavatories reduces this problem, while repeatedly drenching contaminated areas with water also helps.

Earthworms

Earthworms are beneficial to gardens, improving drainage and mixing layers of soil, but when in lawns they produce unsightly and slippery worm casts on the surface, especially during spring and autumn. Brush off or spread the casts and use a proprietary wormkiller.

Moles

Mounds of soil on lawns are unsightly. The tunnels eventually collapse, too, and result in ridges and sunken lines on the surface. Prevention and control must be humane; with persistent mole problems, seek advice from a professional mole catcher. Additionally, pieces of *Euphorbia lathyris* (Caper Spurge, Myrtle Spurge, Mole Plant) deter them.

Ants

They are most prevalent in light and sandy soils, where they loosen and disturb the surface, causing problems when a lawn is mown. Some ants also damage roots, causing brown and yellow areas as grass seedlings wilt. Brush off loose soil and use a proprietary antkiller.

Chafer grubs

Fat, curled and U-shaped, fleshy and plump, dirty, creamy-white larvae chew roots and cause small, brown patches of dying grass. Mainly a problem with lawns newly converted from grassland. Roll lawns in spring to crush the larvae and use a proprietary insecticide.

Adult beetles are shown on page 23.

Leatherjackets

Larvae of the cranefly (daddy-longlegs); tough, leathery-skinned, brownish-grey, legless and about 2.5 cm (1 in) long. Most prevalent in spring and early summer and on lawns newly converted from grassland, feeding on roots and creating patches of yellow or brown grass. Water the area with an insecticide.

Adult

Larva

DISEASES OF LAWNS

Dollar spot

Usually only a problem on fine-leaved turf, especially if it contains Red Fescue. Circular patches, up to 7.5 cm (3 in) across, become yellow-brown or straw-coloured, mostly in mild, wet weather in early autumn. Aerate lawns in autumn and rake off dead grass. Use nitrogen-rich fertilizers only in spring, and apply a fungicide.

Red thread

Prevalent on light or poor soils and those low in nitrogen, especially after the leaching nature of torrential rain. Lawns formed of fine grasses are most at risk. Mostly seen in late summer, with reddish-pink, needle-like growths on leaves. Aerate and feed lawns, especially early in the annual growing cycle, and use a lawn fungicide.

Fusarium *patch*

Also known as 'snow mould', it is widespread in lawns, especially in autumn and on fine-leaved grasses. Deep snow in winter encourages it in spring, but it also occurs in damp, cool conditions from autumn to early spring. Results in yellowish-brown, somewhat circular patches up to 30 cm (1 ft) wide, with grey-white shading. Aerate lawns, avoid high-nitrogen fertilizers and use a lawn fungicide.

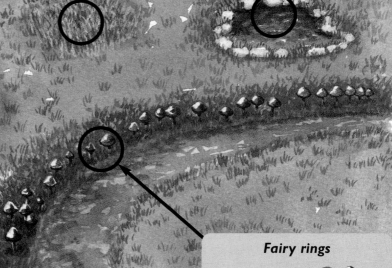

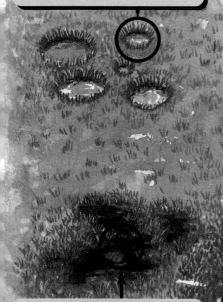

Algae

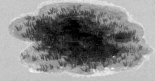

Unsightly black or green slime coats the grass, often occurring under trees that drip water, but also on heavy and consolidated land. Scrape off the slime and remove the algae with a proprietary algicide; thoroughly aerate the lawn and apply a balanced fertilizer in spring.

Fairy rings

Several fungi produce somewhat circular rings of toadstools on lawns; usually the result of buried organic debris. The ring gradually extends outwards, with grass in the centre becoming stunted and yellow. Removing tufts and soil from infected areas is not usually satisfactory as the fungus is wide-spreading. Instead, aerate the turf and apply a balanced fertilizer in spring.

Culinary herbs

Are culinary herbs especially at risk?

Apart from general pests and diseases, culinary herbs have few problems. However, some of the pests that are common to most gardens, such as aphids, slugs and millipedes, can soon devastate herbs if they are not spotted quickly and control measures taken. If you are not growing your herbs organically, take care not to use chemicals that have a long residual period, because these may make the herbs unusable for culinary purposes.

PESTS OF CULINARY HERBS

Earwigs

Throughout summer and into autumn, young and adult earwigs chew ragged holes in leaves and flowers. They hide among plants and rubbish during the day and feed at night. Trap them in straw-filled pots upturned on canes or shallow trays filled with vegetable oil, or use a contact insecticide. Clear away rubbish.

Slugs

These are nature's stealth pests, hiding during the day and devouring plants at night, especially during damp weather. Clear away all rubbish and hiding areas and use slug pellets. Traps and broken eggshells around plants deter them.

Aphids

Both greenfly and blackfly infest herbs, causing distortion and excreting honeydew on leaves and stems, which attracts ants and sooty mould, a black fungus that makes them unsightly and inedible. Spray with a contact insecticide as soon as they are seen.

Caterpillars

Many leaf-eating caterpillars infest culinary herbs, chewing leaves and creating holes. Keep a check on plants and pick off and destroy the caterpillars. Spray with a contact insecticide, but allow time between spraying and harvesting.

Woodlice

Also known as 'pillbugs', 'sowbugs' and 'slaters', these grey, hard-coated pests hide under rubbish during the day and chew plants mainly at night. Remove rubbish and hiding places and use baits to lure and trap them. Dust with a pesticide.

Weevils

Beetle-like and usually with snouts, they produce white, legless grubs. Between them, the beetles and larvae feed on roots, stems, leaves, tubers, corms and flowers. They generally feed at night, hiding during the day. Remove all rubbish and other hiding places. If the infestation is severe, use a contact insecticide.

Flea beetles

Adult beetles chew seedlings in spring and early summer, creating small, round holes in young leaves. The larvae also sometimes chew roots. Attacks are most severe during dry weather, and the beetles are most active on bright, sunny days. Clear away all rubbish under which they can hide, and dust the leaves with an insecticidal dust.

Cutworms

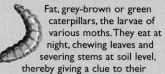

Fat, grey-brown or green caterpillars, the larvae of various moths. They eat at night, chewing leaves and severing stems at soil level, thereby giving a clue to their common name. They are not a major problem but may be present in newly created herb gardens. Remove weeds and use an insecticidal dust.

Chafer grubs

Fat, curled and U-shaped, fleshy and plump, dirty, creamy-white larvae. They are especially a problem on land newly cultivated from grassland. Pick off and destroy adult beetles. Thoroughly dig land when preparing a herb garden, and dust with an insecticide.

Adult beetles are shown on page 23.

Snails

These have the same chewing and rasping nature as slugs and usually feed at night on leaves and stems. They are especially prevalent during damp weather. Pick them off and destroy, or use baits and traps. Usually, they are less of a problem than slugs.

Wireworms

Larvae of the click beetle or 'skip-jack'; they chew roots, stems and tubers and are most prevalent on land newly converted from grassland. Dust the soil with a pesticide. Trapping is possible by shallowly burying cut carrots or potatoes and removing them when contaminated with wireworms.

Millipedes

Both black and snake millipedes damage plants, feeding on roots, bulbs and tubers, often after initial damage has been caused by slugs and wireworms. In autumn, burn all rubbish and when preparing a new bed for culinary herbs cultivate the soil deeply in winter. Dust the soil with an insecticide.

DISEASES OF CULINARY HERBS

Grey mould (Botrytis)

Fluffy, grey mould appears on soft stems, leaves, buds and flowers. It is encouraged by damp and humid conditions, and especially where plants are congested. Cut off and destroy infected parts, increase the circulation of air and use a systemic fungicide.

Mint rust

Stems and leaves initially become pale-coloured and distorted; later, covered with masses of dirty, orange cups. These are followed by yellow, then black, pustules. Pull up and burn infected plants, especially in autumn, and plant only healthy plants.

Soft fruits

What are the main problems?

Because these fruits are relatively soft, they are soon damaged by pests and diseases, as well as by birds, excessive rain and hot weather. Leaves and stems are also at risk from pests and diseases, as well as from other problems including frost, inadequate feeding and old age. For example, strawberry plants soon deteriorate and need replacing every three years. Blackcurrants, if they are pruned annually, will continue to bear fruits for up to 15 years.

AT-A-GLANCE CHECK FOR SOFT FRUITS

Some soft fruits are especially susceptible to specific pests and diseases. Here is a guide to the main pests and diseases to consider when you notice damage, but there are others featured on pages 38–41.

BLACKCURRANTS

RASPBERRIES, BLACKBERRIES AND HYBRID BERRIES

Pests: aphids (greenfly), birds, raspberry beetles. *Diseases:* grey mould (Botrytis), *cane spot, viruses.*

GOOSEBERRIES

Pests: aphids (greenfly), big bud mites, birds, spider mites. *Diseases:* American mildew, grey mould (Botrytis), *leaf spot, reversion.*

Pests: aphids (greenfly), birds, gooseberry sawfly, magpie moths. *Diseases:* American mildew, cluster cup rust, dieback.

GRAPES

REDCURRANTS

Pests: scale insects, spider mites.
Diseases: grey mould (Botrytis), powdery mildew.
Cultural problems: shanking.

Pests: aphids (greenfly), capsid bugs, caterpillars.
Diseases: leaf spot.

WHITECURRANTS

STRAWBERRIES

Pests: aphids (greenfly), birds, slugs and snails.
Diseases: grey mould (Botrytis), strawberry mildew, viruses.

Pests: aphids (greenfly), capsid bugs, caterpillars.
Diseases: leaf spot.

PESTS OF SOFT FRUITS

Blackcurrant leaf midges

Also known as 'blackcurrant gall midges', they are destructive, causing young, terminal shoots to fail to develop and become twisted. Small, white or orange larvae feed on young leaves and shoots. Spray with a contact or systemic insecticide before the first flowers open, and again later, after they fade.

Aphids

Several races of aphids infest soft fruits, including those that cause blistering on leaves and leaf curling. In all cases, spray with a systemic or non-systemic insecticide as soon as the aphids are seen.

Big bud mites

Microscopic in size

Also known as 'blackcurrant gall mites', they cause buds on blackcurrants to swell to twice their normal size. Big bud mites also spread the virus known as 'reversion' (see page 40), which is a serious problem and cannot be cured. Therefore, you should dig up and burn infected bushes in winter.

Scale insects

Several types of scale insects, including brown scale, attack gooseberries, currants and raspberries and are especially prevalent on old and neglected plants. Spray with a tar oil winter-wash. Also spray with a systemic insecticide in spring and autumn.

Currant clearwing moths

Attack black- and redcurrants, as well as gooseberries, and are mainly found on neglected bushes. Moths lay eggs in early summer and their white caterpillars tunnel into stems, causing leaves to wilt and stems to die. Cut out stems to where they are not discoloured; burn all wood that is cut out.

Gooseberry sawfly

Highly damaging to gooseberries, when severe attacks defoliate bushes. Black- and redcurrants are attacked, but to a lesser degree. They initially appear in late spring, infesting the centres of bushes. Pick off caterpillars and spray with a contact insecticide immediately they are seen.

Magpie moths

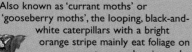

Also known as 'currant moths' or 'gooseberry moths', the looping, black-and-white caterpillars with a bright orange stripe mainly eat foliage on currants, gooseberries and apricots. Often found on neglected bushes and trees. Pick off and burn the caterpillars, or use a contact insecticide.

Birds

They eat buds and tear leaves. Prevention must be humane and fruit cages are the best solution. Alternatively, lay temporary netting over plants to deter them.

Capsid bugs

The common green capsid and apple capsid puncture leaves, sucking sap and injecting toxic saliva and leaving small, ragged holes. Terminal buds may be damaged. They are a particular problem on black- and redcurrants and gooseberries. Clear away and burn winter rubbish, and spray with a systemic or non-systemic insecticide in spring and early summer.

Raspberry beetles

Serious pest of raspberries, blackberries and loganberries. The adult beetles damage blossom, while the small, white grubs chew through fruits, making them inedible. Dust or spray with an insecticide – blackberries just before the first flowers open, and raspberries and loganberries after the flowers fade.

Raspberry moths

The larvae attack the tips of raspberry canes, loganberries and blackberries. In spring, caterpillars bore into shoots, causing them to wither and sometimes to die. Prune plants yearly, and cut back and burn infected shoots. In winter, drench the canes with a tar-oil wash. Keep the bases of plants rubbish-free.

Yellow-tailed moths

Raspberries, as well as apples, pears, cherries, plums and rose bushes, are attacked. The larvae (which can cause a skin rash if touched) skeletonize leaves. Picking off and burning caterpillars is usually all that is needed.

Strawberry tortrix moths

Leaves become encapsulated and joined by silken threads that protect the small, green caterpillars. Chemical control is difficult and the first controlling step is to pick off and burn 'spun' leaves. Using strong jets of water and spraying with an insecticide before plants flower also helps to control them.

Strawberry blossom weevils

Sometimes known as 'elephant beetles', they infest strawberries, raspberries and black-berries. Adult beetles use their snouts to make holes in unopened blossoms, in which eggs are laid. Unopened flowers wither and may fail to open. If damage is serious, spray with a contact insecticide.

Slugs

Strawberries are especially at risk, particularly where fruits are resting directly on the soil, rather than on straw. Use slug baits and traps.

Red-legged weevils

Sometimes known as 'plum weevils', these are a serious pest of strawberries, raspberries, gooseberries and peaches. Adult weevils feed at night, on shoots, buds, blossom and fruitlets, while the legless, white larvae feed on roots. Cultivate and disturb the soil; grease bands and traps help to prevent weevils climbing canes and trees.

Snails

Distinctive and destructive pests that chew and tear fruits and leaves. Use baits and traps.

Spider mites

Several mites infest soft fruits. Strawberry mites are especially troublesome on strawberries, when plants lose vigour and become brittle. Bryobia mites cause progressive discoloration and, ultimately, defoliation, on fruits such as gooseberries, apples and pears. Red spider mites infest strawberries and blackcurrants, especially in hot summers.

DISEASES AND PHYSIOLOGICAL PROBLEMS OF SOFT FRUITS

Reversion

Serious virus of blackcurrants. Leaves cease to have five clear lobes and five or more veins on each side of the main lobe. Yields of fruits slowly diminish. Big bud mites (see page 38) spread the virus. Dig up and burn seriously infected plants, and plant only clean, virus-free plants.

Leaf spot

Sometimes known as 'currant leaf spot', it is a serious disease of blackcurrants (also infecting gooseberries and red- and whitecurrants) with small, irregular, brownish spots or blotches on leaves. Plants eventually become defoliated. Pick off and burn diseased leaves and spray with a fungicide as soon as the problem is seen.

Blackcurrant rust

Pernicious problem of blackcurrants, with undersides of leaves assuming yellow patches in early summer. Later, leaves turn brown and often fall. Immediately the fruits are picked, spray with a fungicide.

Gooseberry cluster cup rust

Mainly a disease of gooseberries, occasionally blackcurrants, when raised, orange-red pustules appear mainly on lower leaves in spring and early summer. Infection sometimes spreads to fruits and is especially prevalent in wet seasons. Dig up and burn seriously infected bushes and replant at wider spacings to increase the air circulation. Do not plant near sedges.

Dieback

Frequently seen on gooseberries and causes the death of young shoots. A grey, mould-like fungus appears on leaves, which wilt and turn first yellow, then brown. Completely cut out infected stems or dig up and burn seriously infected plants.

American gooseberry mildew

Serious disease of gooseberries (not to be confused with European gooseberry mildew), resulting in a white, powdery coating (later pale brown) on leaves, shoots and fruits. Encouraged by congestion and lack of air circulation. Cut off infected branches in early autumn and spray with a fungicide in the following year.

Powdery mildew

Fungi create a white, powdery coating on leaves (usually both surfaces) and stems, and may also infect flowers and fruits. Burn infected leaves and spray with a fungicide as soon as the problem is noticed.

Shanking

Physiological disorder of grapes, causing entire berries to shrivel. Complete bunches of fruit are affected. It is caused by excessive cropping or soil problems, including poor feeding and dry soil caused by irregular and uneven watering. Thin bunches of grapes and ensure that they are at least 25 cm (10 in) apart.

Raspberry spur blight

Fungal disease of raspberries and loganberries, first noticed as purplish patches on canes in early autumn (infection is earlier). Immediately cut out infected canes to below soil level, burn them and reduce the number of young canes to increase air circulation around them. Spray remaining canes with a fungicide.

Grey mould (Botrytis)

Fruits of strawberries, raspberries and grapes (and currants in especially wet seasons) become covered in a grey, fluffy mould that makes them inedible. Especially prevalent in wet summers. Remove berries and cut out infected canes. Avoid overcrowding the canes and spray with a fungicide when the first flowers open.

Strawberry powdery mildew

Serious disease, with dark patches on upper surfaces of leaves and curling at their edges, revealing white, floury areas on the undersides. Fruits become dull-coloured, inedible and, usually, shrivelled. Burn infected leaves and spray with a fungicide.

Viruses

Pernicious, destructive and especially a problem with strawberries and raspberries. Vigour decreases and leaves become distorted and crinkled, assuming yellow patterns or streaks. Sap-sucking insects, such as aphids, transmit viruses. Burn infected plants, spray against sap-sucking insects and buy only clean plants.

Cane spot

Fungus disease, affecting raspberries, loganberries and hybrid berries. First seen in early summer, when small, purple spots enlarge to create shallow, sunken, white areas encircled in purple. In autumn, cut out and burn badly diseased canes and in the following spring use a fungicide. The old raspberry variety 'Lloyd George' is especially susceptible to this disease.

Tree fruits

Problems with tree fruits encompass damage to fruits, blossom, leaves, stems and bark. Some of these are just unsightly, while others make fruits inedible or unable to be stored for use later in the year. Damage is caused by insects and diseases, as well as by physiological disorders. To complicate matters, pests often initially damage fruits, allowing diseases to enter later and cause further damage. Never store fruits that have become bruised or damaged by pests and diseases.

What should I look out for?

AT-A-GLANCE CHECK FOR TREE FRUITS

Some tree fruits are especially susceptible to specific pests and diseases. Here is a guide to the main pests and diseases to consider when damage is noticed, but there are others described on pages 44–53.

APRICOTS

Pests: aphids (greenfly), red spider mites.
Diseases: bacterial canker, dieback, silver leaf.

APPLES

Pests: aphids (greenfly), caterpillars, codling moths.
Diseases: brown rot, canker, mildew, scab.

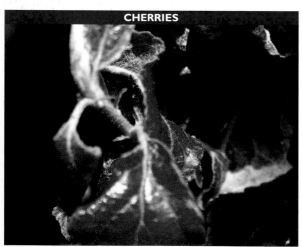

CHERRIES

Pests: birds, blackfly.
Diseases: bacterial canker, brown rot, silver leaf.

FIGS

Pests: aphids (greenfly).
Diseases: canker, coral spot, grey mould (Botrytis).

PEACHES AND NECTARINES

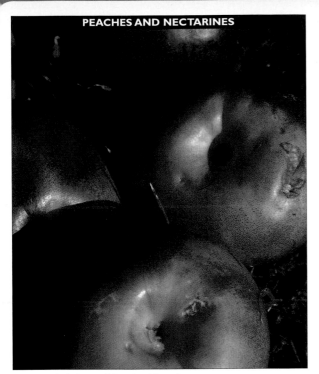

Pests: aphids (greenfly), red spider mites.
Diseases: bacterial canker, peach leaf curl, silver leaf.

PEARS

Pests: aphids (greenfly), caterpillars, pear and cherry slugworms.
Diseases: fireblight, scab.

PLUMS

Pests: aphids (greenfly), birds, red spider mites, plum sawfly, wasps.
Diseases: brown rot, silver leaf.

QUINCES

Pests: aphids (greenfly)
Diseases: brown rot, mildew.

PESTS OF TREE FRUITS

Codling moths

Serious pest of apples and occasionally pears, quinces and plums. Caterpillars enter fruits, feed during mid- and late summer and produce sawdust-like 'frass'. They then leave the fruits, spin cocoons and hide under loose bark. In mid-summer, tie sacking or corrugated cardboard around trunks to trap overwintering caterpillars. Spray with an insecticide after blossoming, and again three weeks later.

Apple blossom weevils

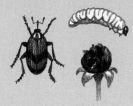

Troublesome on apples and occasionally pears and quinces. Blossoms do not open ('capped'), petals die and flower buds turn brown. Inside, there is a cream-coloured larva, yellowish pupa, or young weevil. Spray with an insecticide just before the flower buds open.

Apple sawfly

Widespread pest of apples. In spring, adult flies lay eggs on the blossom. Creamy-white grubs tunnel under the skin of small fruitlets, causing ribbon-like scars, then burrow to the centre and produce sticky 'frass'. Fruits drop from trees. Spray with an insecticide a week after the petals fall; pick up and burn infected fruits.

Apple leaf skeletonizer

Serious pest of apples, pears and cherries in some areas. Occasionally, peaches are affected. Small, greenish-yellow caterpillars, spotted black and with a yellow stripe, skeletonize small areas of leaves, which curl at their edges. Pick off caterpillars and spray with a contact insecticide.

Apple capsid bugs

Serious pest, and similar to the common green capsid bug, they puncture newly developed leaves and suck sap, initially creating brownish-black spots, which later become ragged. Young fruitlets become pitted, corky and distorted, with russetting and cracking. Spray with a contact or systemic insecticide in spring.

Caterpillars

Several moths decimate leaves and petals, including the mottled umber moth and the winter moth; they mainly feed in spring. Pick off and destroy, use grease bands and spray with a contact insecticide. The vapourer moth feeds slightly later.

Vapourer moth

Mottled umber moth

Fruit tree tortrix moths

Apples, pears, plums, cherries, apricots, blackberries and raspberries are affected. Either the edges of leaves are spun together, or leaves are attached to fruits. Caterpillars characteristically wriggle backwards when disturbed and may drop down on a silken thread. Pick off caterpillars and spun leaves and drench with a contact insecticide.

Woolly aphids

Infest apples, as well as ornamental crab apples and pears, *Pyracantha* and *Cotoneaster*. Sometimes known as 'American blight', colonies of aphids secrete masses of white, wool-like wax that cling to shoots and branches. Roots are sometimes infested. Use a small brush and methylated spirits to remove small infestations. Also spray with a contact or systemic insecticide.

Pear and cherry slugworms

Also known as 'pear and cherry sawfly', they mainly infest pears and cherries and, occasionally, apples, plums and quinces. The slug-like larvae feed on the upper surfaces of leaves, often 'skeletonizing' them. Spray with a contact insecticide.

Birds

Birds can be troublesome, with bullfinches eating flower buds of plums, pears, cherries, gooseberries and many ornamental plants; blackbirds and tits peck young fruits on apples and pears; sparrows attack apple blossom. Fruit cages over small trees and temporary netting are two solutions.

Cherry blackfly

Pernicious insects, infesting ornamental as well as fruiting cherries. Infested young shoots and leaves become stunted and distorted. The blackfly excrete honeydew, which attracts ants and encourages the presence of sooty mould. Spray with a systemic or non-systemic insecticide in spring.

PESTS OF TREE FRUITS (CONTINUED)

Pear leaf midges

Also known as 'leaf midges' and 'pear leaf-curling midges', but not to be confused with pear midges (see right), these especially cause the edges of young pear leaves to roll or curl upwards and inwards. Pick off and burn affected leaves. The cloistered grubs are difficult to control by spraying.

Pear midges

More serious than pear leaf midges, these are a common problem with pears. The larvae attack young pear fruitlets, causing them to become larger, then black and deformed and, usually, to fall. Pears growing against walls are most at risk. Pick off and burn infected fruits and spray with a contact insecticide. Pick up and burn fruits that have fallen.

Winter moths

Pernicious pest of apples, pears, cherries and black- and redcurrants. Caterpillars of the winter moth mainly devour young leaves, but may also feed on flower stalks, petals and even fruitlets. Caterpillars have a looping gait. Install grease bands in early autumn. If the infestation is serious, spray with a contact insecticide.

Lackey moths

One of a group of moths with caterpillars that form 'tents' of silken webs, known as 'tent' caterpillars. They infest apples, pears, plums, cherries and many ornamental shrubs and trees. They feed on leaves, often causing complete defoliation. If possible, cut out and burn infected shoots and leaves, and spray with a contact insecticide.

Apple leafhoppers

Several leafhoppers infest apples; they are related to aphids, feeding on plants and jumping and flying off when disturbed. Young leafhoppers feed on the undersides of leaves, causing pale and mottled patches. Spray with a contact or systemic insecticide.

Apple aphids

Several races of aphids infest apple trees, as well as pears, plums and peaches. They pierce leaves and other parts, sucking sap and causing debilitation and deformation. They also transmit viruses and encourage the presence of ants and sooty mould. Spray with a contact or systemic insecticide.

Pear leaf blister mites

Usually infest wall-trained and cordon pears; young leaves initially spotted with yellow markings that turn to blackish blisters; the leaves then fall. Young fruits may become blistered. Pick off and burn affected leaves and fruitlets. Chemical control is not feasible for home gardeners.

Tent caterpillars

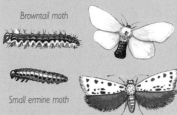

Browntail moth

Small ermine moth

As well as those of lackey moths (see opposite page), other 'tent' caterpillars include the browntail moth and small ermine moth, which are most harmful on apple trees, as well as pears, plums and cherries. They feed on leaves, often causing complete defoliation. If possible, cut out and burn infected shoots and leaves, and spray with a contact insecticide.

Wasps

Most troublesome in late summer and early autumn, when they damage ripening fruits of plums, apples and pears, as well as peaches, nectarines, apricots, grapes and figs. Wasps live in nests and their populations vary from one season to another. Destroy the nest with a proprietary waspkiller. Alternatively, call in a pest-control specialist to deal with the problem.

Plum sawfly

Similar to apple sawfly, but only affects plums and damsons. Caterpillars tunnel into young fruits, creating a mass of sticky, black 'frass' around the entrance hole. The creamy-white larvae feed within the fruit, causing them to fall. Pick up and burn infected fruits, and spray with a contact insecticide just after the petals fall.

Fruit tree red spider mites

Serious problem, especially on apples, pears, plums and damsons. Microscopic, eight-legged, spider-like creatures infest the lower leaf surfaces and initially cause light mottling and speckling on their upper surfaces; later, they turn bronze, become brittle and eventually die. Spray with an acaricide (see page 78).

Scale

Neglected trees in orchards are most likely to have scale; there are several types, but oystershell scale (illustrated) and mussel scale are most likely. They infect all types of tree fruits; where possible, cut off and burn badly affected shoots and branches, or spray with a winter-wash.

DISEASES AND PHYSIOLOGICAL DISORDERS OF TREE FRUITS

Dieback

General term for the death of young shoots on trees and shrubs, both fruiting and ornamental. It usually results from diseases entering wounds earlier created by insects or through physical damage, perhaps from severe frost. Cut back infected shoots to healthy tissue. It is more common in stone fruits, such as cherries, than apples and pears.

Fireblight

Bacterial disease, devastating on pears and apples as well many ornamental plants. Bacteria enter the flowers, which turn black, then spread. Leaves wither and often fail to fall, while affected shoots wilt and die. Once the trunk is affected the tree dies. Cut out and burn diseased wood to at least 60 cm (2 ft) below the infection. It is a notifiable disease (see page 78).

Apple powdery mildew

Powdery mildew infects apples, pears, medlars and quinces. White or grey powdery coating on leaves, shoots and, occasionally, buds and flowers. It makes an appearance in spring from fungus that has overwintered on shoots and in bud scales. In winter, cut out and burn infected shoots and spray with a fungicide during spring and summer. Varieties such as 'Cox's Orange Pippin' and 'Lane's Prince Albert' are especially susceptible.

Shot hole disease

Fungal disease of cherries, nectarines, peaches and plums that initially produces brown spots that later fall away to reveal holes. Poorly fed and weak trees, especially during dry weather, are susceptible; therefore, regularly feed trees.

Silver leaf disease

Fungal disease that infects cherries, peaches, nectarines, almonds, apricots, apples and plums. Fungus enters trees through wounds or pruning cuts, with leaves developing a silvery sheen. Cross-sections of infected branches reveal purple and brown staining. Prune these at-risk fruits only in late spring or early summer – not in winter. Cut back infected branches (coating cut surfaces with a fungicidal paint), and grub out and burn seriously diseased trees.

Peach leaf curl

Notorious fungal disease of peaches, nectarines, almonds and apricots. Foliage assumes a reddish flush; then large, reddish blisters, later covered in white spores, appear; leaves curl and fall, and the tree is weakened. Collect and burn infected leaves. Spray with a fungicide in autumn, late winter and early spring.

SPRAYING PEARS

When spraying pears (as well as apples) with insecticides and fungicides, it is essential not to spray trees when they are in blossom and pollinating insects are flying. For pears, this is the latter part of mid-spring and into early late spring. This is slightly earlier than for apples, but times for all fruits vary from area to area.

WHITE BUD STAGE   **PETAL FALL STAGE**   **FRUITLET STAGE**

Spraying routine
Here are the main times to spray pears.
• Winter (early and mid-winter)
• Green cluster stage (early spring)

• White bud stage (mid-spring)
• Petal fall stage (mid- and late spring)
• Fruitlet stage (middle part of early summer to middle part of mid-summer)

DISEASES AND PHYSIOLOGICAL DISORDERS OF TREE FRUITS (CONTINUED)

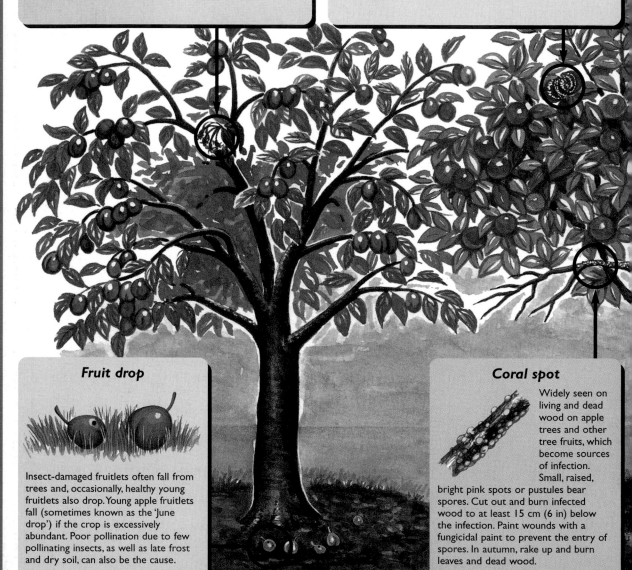

Blossom wilt

Fungal disease, related to brown rot, with the blossom wilting and turning brown. Plums, as well as apples and pears, are affected and it is mostly seen on old trees and in neglected orchards. Remove infected blossom, complete with dead twigs. It mainly occurs during mild, wet springs. Regularly spray trees to prevent insect attack and to control fungal diseases.

Brown rot

Fungal disease, mainly affecting apples but also pears, peaches, nectarines, cherries, plums, quinces, medlars and apricots. Soft brown patches appear on fruits, often initiated by insect and physical damage. Fruits turn brown, with concentric rings of yellowish mould; later, fruits shrink and become mummified. Prevent insect damage by regularly spraying trees, and store only undamaged fruits.

Fruit drop

Insect-damaged fruitlets often fall from trees and, occasionally, healthy young fruitlets also drop. Young apple fruitlets fall (sometimes known as the 'June drop') if the crop is excessively abundant. Poor pollination due to few pollinating insects, as well as late frost and dry soil, can also be the cause.

Coral spot

Widely seen on living and dead wood on apple trees and other tree fruits, which become sources of infection. Small, raised, bright pink spots or pustules bear spores. Cut out and burn infected wood to at least 15 cm (6 in) below the infection. Paint wounds with a fungicidal paint to prevent the entry of spores. In autumn, rake up and burn leaves and dead wood.

Apple and pear canker

Fungal disease that attacks apples and pears. The fungus enters through wounds created by pests and results in small, elongated, sunken, puckered patches around them. Cracks and other small wounds in the bark give access to the fungus. Young shoots and branches may be killed. Cut off and burn affect shoots and branches. Regularly spray with insecticides to prevent insect damage, and use a fungicide.

Apple scab

Pernicious fungal disease of apples; a similar fungus attacks pears. The disease overwinters on fallen leaves and young shoots, is most severe after a wet and late spring, and first appears as small black spots on young fruitlets. These develop into dark-coloured, corky scabs. Young leaves become peppered with somewhat round, greenish-brown spots. Spray in spring, as well as later (see page 53).

Blossom drop

Sometimes trees lose their flowers without any fruit setting. Some fruits need a suitable pollinating partner nearby to provide pollen. Additionally, late spring frosts sometimes damage blossom, while cold and wet springs influence opportunities for pollinating insects to fly and pollinate flowers.

Bitter pit

Disorder of apples, occurring on half-grown fruits or when they are in store. A similar disorder affects pears and quinces. Small, dark spots appear just beneath the fruit's skin, which develop into small depressions. Fruits become bitter and inedible. Fluctuating soil moisture, calcium deficiency and high nitrogen levels influence its presence. Apply a balanced fertilizer in spring.

Crown gall

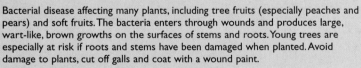

Bacterial disease affecting many plants, including tree fruits (especially peaches and pears) and soft fruits. The bacteria enters through wounds and produces large, wart-like, brown growths on the surfaces of stems and roots. Young trees are especially at risk if roots and stems have been damaged when planted. Avoid damage to plants, cut off galls and coat with a wound paint.

Storage rot

Apples, as well as other fruits, rot when in store if they have been mechanically damaged or weakened through pest attacks. Regularly spray trees and bushes against pests, and store only healthy fruits. Remember to check them every week and remove those that show signs of infection. See also brown rot, opposite.

Prevention and control for fruits

Is regular spraying necessary?

In some seasons and in a few locations, especially those where only a few soft fruits or tree fruits are grown and where there has not been a build-up of pests and diseases, it may not be necessary to adopt a regular spraying programme. Where these fruits are grown in numbers and concentrated in one area, however, keen fruit growers invariably spray at specific times through the year to prevent problems occurring.

YEAR-ROUND CARE

Apart from identifying pests and diseases (the major problems with soft and tree fruits are illustrated and described on pages 36–51), knowing when to spray and the chemicals to choose are equally important. This need not be complicated, and combined chemical sprays for controlling insects and disease are available from garden centres and garden stores. The best times to use them are described and illustrated on the opposite page for apples, and on page 49 for pears.

When pollinating insects are flying, spraying should be avoided; these times are mainly when flowers are open (see opposite page and page 49). When using a chemical spray, choose the latter part of the day when fewer beneficial insects are flying and bees are not active. Remember, too, that it is far better to encourage the presence of beneficial insects and animals in gardens than to rely on the use of chemicals (see pages 6–7 for details of beneficial insects).

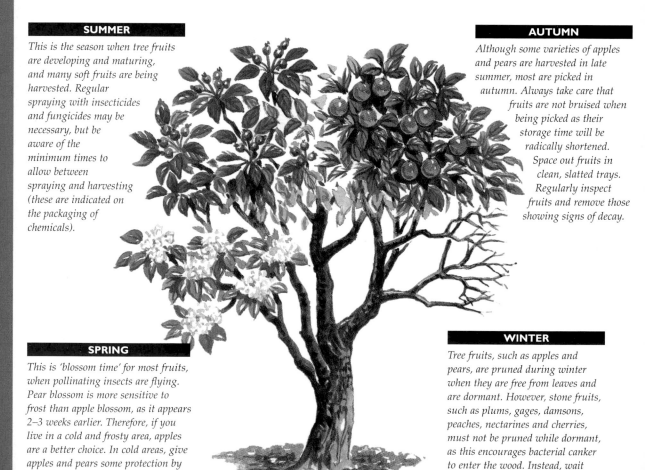

SUMMER

This is the season when tree fruits are developing and maturing, and many soft fruits are being harvested. Regular spraying with insecticides and fungicides may be necessary, but be aware of the minimum times to allow between spraying and harvesting (these are indicated on the packaging of chemicals).

AUTUMN

Although some varieties of apples and pears are harvested in late summer, most are picked in autumn. Always take care that fruits are not bruised when being picked as their storage time will be radically shortened. Space out fruits in clean, slatted trays. Regularly inspect fruits and remove those showing signs of decay.

SPRING

This is 'blossom time' for most fruits, when pollinating insects are flying. Pear blossom is more sensitive to frost than apple blossom, as it appears 2–3 weeks earlier. Therefore, if you live in a cold and frosty area, apples are a better choice. In cold areas, give apples and pears some protection by growing them against a sheltered and sun-facing wall.

WINTER

Tree fruits, such as apples and pears, are pruned during winter when they are free from leaves and are dormant. However, stone fruits, such as plums, gages, damsons, peaches, nectarines and cherries, must not be pruned while dormant, as this encourages bacterial canker to enter the wood. Instead, wait until their sap is rising in late spring or early summer.

WHEN TO SPRAY APPLE TREES

The spraying times for apples are slightly later than for pears, but often vary from one area to another.

Spraying routine
• Winter (early and mid-winter)
• Bud burst to green cluster stage (mid-spring)
• Pink bud stage (latter part of mid-spring)
• Petal fall stage (late spring)
• Fruitlet stage (middle part of early summer to middle part of mid-summer)

BUD BURST STAGE

GREEN CLUSTER STAGE

PINK BUD STAGE

PETAL FALL STAGE

FRUITLET STAGE

WHAT IS CANKER?

Often used as a general term for any wound on trees and shrubs and closely associated with shoots that die back, canker is a destructive problem on gooseberries and cherries (see 'Dieback', pages 40 and 48), as well as on other plants. Fireblight, a related and devastating disease of apples and pears, is described on page 48.

Cankers

Like dieback, cankers are serious and if neglected eventually damage (and may kill) the whole tree.
• **Apple and pear canker** is featured on page 51.
• **Bacterial canker** is a serious problem with plums (usually on main stems) and cherries (on branches and in crotches), as well as on peaches, nectarines, almonds and apricots. It also affects ornamental cherry trees. It mostly attacks young trees, but also established ones. The bacteria live on the foliage and the first sign of an impending problem is pale-edged spots on the leaves. In autumn, infections are splashed onto stems and enter the plant through leaf scars (where leaves were earlier joined to the branch) or wounds made by insects, as well as through pruning cuts made at the wrong time of the year. At first, affected areas are shallow or flat, with amber-coloured gum exuding from the wood and covering the area. If left unattended, the branch or stem eventually

dies. If it occurs on the trunk (perhaps through tree-ties rubbing the bark), the entire tree will eventually die. Cut out infected branches in summer, when the rising sap has an opportunity to prevent infection getting into the tree. Ensure that all cuts are coated in a fungicidal paint. Spray with a fungicide in late summer or early autumn to prevent infection getting into the tree.

← *Small, pale-edged spots on leaves are the first signs of bacterial canker*

→ *Infected plum branches produce few leaves, with distinctive amber-coloured gum oozing from the cankers*

← *With cherries, cankers exuding gum may appear on the branches as well as in the crotches of branches*

Vegetables

Are all vegetables at risk?

Most vegetables are susceptible to pests and diseases at some time during their growth, although those with a harvesting period that falls mainly during winter are less at risk. Growing large areas of similar vegetables attracts a build-up of the same pests and diseases; therefore you should regularly inspect plants and spray as soon as problems are noticed. Aphids (greenfly) are omnipresent, especially during late spring and summer.

BEETROOT

Pests: aphids (greenfly), black bean aphids, mangold fly. Diseases: black leg. Cultural problems: bolting, fanging, heart rot.

BRASSICAS (Brussels sprouts, cabbages and cauliflowers)

Pests: cabbage root fly, cabbage stem flea beetles, cabbage whitefly, caterpillars, chafer grubs, cutworms, diamond-back moths, flea beetles, pigeons, slugs, snails. Diseases: clubroot, downy mildew, leaf spot. Cultural problems: blown Brussels sprouts, heartless cabbages, whiptail.

CARROTS AND PARSNIPS

Pests: carrot fly, swift moths. Diseases: black rot, carrot root rot (Sclerotinia rot), parsnip canker, violet root rot. Cultural problems: fanging, splitting.

CELERY

Pests: celery leaf miners, slugs, snails. Diseases: celery heart rot, celery leaf spot.

CUCURBITS (Courgettes/zucchinis, cucumbers, marrows, pumpkins, squashes)

Pests: eelworms, red spider mites, slugs, snails. Diseases: basal stem rot, cucumber mosaic virus, grey mould (Botrytis), powdery mildew, root rot, stem rot.

LETTUCES

Pests: aphids (greenfly), cutworms, eelworms, root aphids, slugs, snails. *Diseases:* downy mildew, grey mould (Botrytis), ring spot. *Cultural problems:* bolting, tip burn.

ONIONS AND LEEKS

Pests: onion fly, stem and bulb eelworms. *Diseases:* downy mildew, neck rot, rust, smut, white rot (mouldy nose), white tip. *Cultural problems:* bolting, bull neck, saddleback.

PEAS AND BEANS

Pests: birds, black bean aphids, pea moths, pea and bean weevils, pea thrips. *Diseases:* anthracnose, chocolate spot, downy mildew, Fusarium wilt, grey mould (Botrytis), halo blight, powdery mildew.

POTATOES

Pests: aphids (greenfly), capsid bugs, potato cyst eelworms, rosy rustic moths, slugs, snails, wireworms. *Diseases:* leaf-roll virus, mosaic virus, potato blight, potato scab, potato wart disease, powdery scab. *Cultural problems:* splitting.

RADISHES, TURNIPS AND SWEDES

Pests: cabbage root fly, flea beetles. *Diseases:* black rot, clubroot.

SPINACH

Pests: slugs, snails. *Diseases:* downy mildew, leaf spot, spinach blight. *Cultural problems:* bolting.

TOMATOES

Pests: eelworms, greenhouse whitefly. *Diseases:* grey mould (Botrytis), tomato leaf mould, tomato foot rot. *Cultural problems:* blossom drop, blossom end rot, blotchy ripening, buckeye rot, dry set, sun scald.

When to spray

When you are choosing a particular insecticide or fungicide to use to prevent or eliminate a problem, check that there is sufficient time between spraying and harvesting for the effects of the chemical to be eliminated. This period will be indicated on the chemical's packaging.

PESTS OF STEMS AND LEAVES OF VEGETABLES

Earwigs

Pernicious pest, chewing ragged holes in leaves of many vegetables, mostly at night. Trapping in pots filled with straw and inverted on the tops of canes helps to remove them, as well as spraying with a contact insecticide. Remove rubbish under which they can hide.

Aphids (greenfly)

From spring to autumn (sometimes longer) these insects infest vegetables, sucking sap and spreading viruses. They also excrete honeydew, which attracts ants, and the black, unsightly sooty mould, which blocks pores in leaves. Spray with an insecticide as soon as they are seen.

Flea beetles

Active pests, especially on bright, sunny days in mid- and late spring, when they eat small, circular holes in seedlings and young leaves on vegetables such as cabbages, turnips, swedes (rutabagas) and radishes. Dust seedlings with an insecticide, use seeds dressed with an insecticide, and clear away and burn all rubbish.

Cabbage caterpillars

Large cabbage white

Small cabbage white

Cabbage moth

Several species of caterpillar (of the large and small cabbage white butterflies) eat leaves of cabbages and related plants, while those of the cabbage moth burrow into the hearts of cabbages, especially in early summer. Check undersides of leaves for the presence of larvae (indicated by adults fluttering over plants) and remove. Also spray with a contact insecticide.

Diamond-back moths

Small, green caterpillars, initially feeding on undersides of cabbage leaves, as well as cauliflowers, broccoli, swedes (rutabagas) and turnips. Later, they eat through to the upper surface. When disturbed, the caterpillars hang from leaves by a silken thread. When seen, use a contact insecticide or a bacterial-type spray based on *Bacillus thuringiensis*.

Birds

Many birds are present in gardens and a few are damaging to vegetables. Woodpigeons are especially destructive to cabbages and other brassicas; they are difficult to deter because they are attracted to readily available food. The only solution is to use a wire cage.

Asparagus beetles

Distinctive beetles with black bodies and yellow-orange squares along their sides. Grubs and adult beetles attack leaves and stems from late spring onwards. Beetles can sometimes be picked off and burned. Spray with a non-persistent insecticide.

Celery leaf miners

Sometimes known as celery fly, these pernicious insects have white larvae that tunnel into leaves, causing blistering, then browning and shrivelling. Inspect plants in spring and early summer and squash larvae in mined leaves. Ensure infested seedlings are not planted and use a contact or systemic insecticide to protect young plants.

Black bean aphids

Mainly attack broad (fava) beans, but also French beans, runner beans, spinach, turnips, parsnips, beet and rhubarb. Black aphids cluster on stems and leaves, sucking sap, transmitting viruses and causing debilitation. With broad (fava) beans, nip out growing points in early summer. Spray with a contact or systemic insecticide, but not when beans are flowering because pollinating insects may be killed.

Swift moths

Several types of these moths and their larvae feed on the roots of vegetables, especially parsnips and carrots, as well as ornamental plants (see page 15). Unlike cutworms, they feed almost totally below ground. They are most prevalent on newly cultivated land. Dust soil with a insecticide and burn infected roots.

Carrot fly

Mainly affect carrots, but also parsnips, celery and parsley. Roots are damaged by small, cream-white maggots, and the initial signs of attack are leaves turning reddish and wilting when in full sun. Impossible to control once plants are infested. Therefore, clear away and burn all rubbish in autumn, sow seeds sparingly to reduce the need for thinning and clear away all thinnings. Position plants with overpowering redolence, such as onions, either side of carrot rows to cloak their aroma.

PESTS OF STEMS AND LEAVES OF VEGETABLES (CONTINUED)

Pea and bean weevils

Pests of peas and broad (fava) beans, also *Lathyrus* (Sweet Peas). Adult weevils eat the edges of leaves, producing U-shaped notching. Growing points are also damaged, especially in spring, with young plants suffering more than older ones, especially in dry weather. Hoe around plants in spring and remove and burn rubbish in winter. Dust with an insecticide when an attack is first seen.

Pea thrips

Pests of peas and broad (fava) beans, as well as *Lathyrus* (Sweet Peas). Pods, as well as flowers and leaves, become misshapen, discoloured and reveal silver mottling. Plants become stunted, with limited flowering and reduced pod production. Damage is worse in hot and dry weather. Remove and burn infected plants in autumn, and spray with a contact insecticide.

Pea moths

Serious pests of garden peas and responsible for 'maggoty' peas. Pale yellow caterpillars, with black heads and legs, lay eggs near young, developing pods. Larvae hatch, enter pods and feed and destroy the peas. About a week after flowering, spray with a contact insecticide, and again 14 days later.

Greenhouse whitefly

Also known as 'glasshouse whitefly'. Although mainly pests of greenhouse plants, they infest outdoor plants in warm and sheltered areas. Especially prevalent on tomato plants, both indoors and outdoors. Resemble minute, white moths; they suck sap, creating honeydew and encouraging the presence of sooty mould. Spray with a contact or systemic insecticide as soon as they are seen.

Onion fly

Serious pests of onions, as well as shallots and leeks. Larvae feed in bulbs and stems, with young plants wilting and dying. If attack is severe, bulbs become soft and rotten. The flies are attracted by the scent of crushed onion leaves; sow seeds sparingly to reduce need to thin seedlings. Lift and burn seriously infected bulbs. Cultivate soil in winter and grow onions from sets if attack is expected.

Stem and bulb eelworms

Sometimes known as 'stem eelworms', these microscopic pests infest onions, daffodils and tulips. Foliage becomes swollen and distorted. Young bulbs are killed, while older ones become soft and unusable. Pull up and burn infected plants and do not grow susceptible plants on the same land for three years.

Rosy rustic moths

Caterpillars hollow out stems of potatoes and top growth soon dies. Gardens newly converted from meadowland are most at risk. Dig up and burn infected plants and dust the soil with a soil insecticide.

Potato cyst eelworms

Serious pests of potatoes (also tomatoes). Endemic in some soils, young eelworms invade roots, causing round, white, yellow or brown cysts on roots. Plants become stunted; leaves turn yellow, then brown, and eventually die. Tubers are small and few in number. Remove and burn infected plants and do not grow potatoes or tomatoes on infected land for eight or more years. Some varieties of potatoes are resistant.

Common green capsid bugs

These capsids puncture leaves, suck sap and inject toxic saliva into plants, leaving small, brown spots that later turn into ragged holes. Vegetables attacked include potatoes and runner beans. Leaflets are chiefly damaged. Clear up rubbish in winter and spray with a systemic or non-systemic insecticide when they are most active, during spring and early summer.

Mangold fly

Also known as 'beet fly', 'leaf miners' and 'beet leaf miners', these pests affect leaves of beetroot and spinach. During late spring and early summer, larvae tunnel into leaves, causing blistering; leaves become brown and growth is retarded. Pick off affected leaves and spray with a systemic insecticide. Clear away and burn all rubbish during winter.

Red spider mites

Primarily found in greenhouses, these pests also occur outdoors and can be especially damaging in hot, dry summers. Vegetables affected include tomatoes, beans, aubergines (eggplants) and capsicums (sweet peppers). The mites habit undersides of leaves and, initially, cause mottling (later yellow and bronze) on the upper surfaces, followed by leaf fall. Spray with an acaricide (see page 78), regularly mist-spray plants (if possible) and pull up and burn all plant debris in autumn or winter.

Root aphids

Also known as 'lettuce root aphids', these infest roots, covering them in white, mealy patches. Plants wilt, become yellow and eventually die. Especially damaging in dry weather and in late summer. For mild infestations, apply a contact insecticide as a soil drench. Pull up and burn badly affected plants and grow varieties, such as 'Avoncrisp' and 'Avondefiance', which are resistant to the aphids.

DISEASES OF STEMS, LEAVES AND ROOTS OF VEGETABLES

Lettuce downy mildew

Common disease of lettuces, outdoors and in greenhouses. Large, pale green or yellowish areas develop on upper leaf surfaces, with a white, downy mould beneath. These areas turn brown and die. Remove and burn seriously infected plants; spray with a fungicide if infection is slight. Do not grow further lettuces on the same area for several years.

Powdery mildew

Affects many plants, including garden peas. Powdery, white coating, first seen on leaves (on both sides) soon spreads to stems and other parts. Especially prevalent in hot, dry seasons. Spray with a fungicide when first seen, with repeat sprayings. After harvesting, pull up and burn infected plants.

Anthracnose of dwarf beans

Seen on dwarf beans, and occasionally runner beans. Usually appears in wet, cold seasons, mainly on leaves and pods but sometimes all parts, as brown, sunken areas. Later, they turn pale pink and entire areas become slimy. Some varieties of dwarf beans are resistant. Burn seriously infected plants and spray others with a fungicide. Rotate crops.

Grey mould (Botrytis)

Often seen on peas and beans, when it coats pods and leaves (later, often on stems) in a grey, fluffy mould. Pick off and burn infected pods and spray with a fungicide to prevent spread.

Bean chocolate spot

A fungal disease of broad (fava) beans, especially during wet seasons and where plants are overcrowded. Long, brown streaks appear on stems, while chocolate-coloured spots pepper leaves, mainly on upper leaf surfaces. Eventually, pods become infected, beans discolour and plants die. Burn seriously infected plants and spray others with a fungicide.

Bean halo blight

Seed-borne bacterial disease, infecting both dwarf and runner beans. Leaves develop water-soaked areas, with characteristic narrow areas around them. Later, stems and pods are infected. Attack is worse in wet seasons; yields are reduced. Lift and burn infected plants, rotate crops and never soak seeds in water before sowing.

Fusarium wilt

Fungal disease, causing stems to wilt. In vegetable plots it is sometimes seen on dwarf and runner beans and garden peas, resulting in stunted growth, rolled or yellowing leaves and a poor crop. Characteristically, stems when cut have reddish-brown streaks. Pull up and burn infected plants, grow wilt-resistant varieties and rotate crops.

Mosaic virus

Several viruses affect potatoes, including mosaic virus, which causes green leaves to show yellow or pale green mottling or spotting. Once plants are infected, little can be done. Buy 'seed' potatoes free from viruses. Also, spray against sap-sucking insects, such as aphids.

Potato blight

Notorious fungal disease of potatoes and, occasionally, tomatoes. Small, black or brown spots appear on leaves, becoming larger and forming a black mass. Tubers become infected and ruined. Plant clean 'seed' potatoes, keep rows earthed up and spray with a fungicide as a preventative measure in mid-summer if weather is damp. Cut down and burn foliage about ten days before harvesting.

Potato leaf roll virus

Virus of potatoes; edges of upper leaflets are rolled inwards. Leaves become brittle and hard, while plants become stunted and yields are poor. Once plants are infected, little can be done. Buy 'seed' potatoes free from viruses. Also spray against sap-sucking insects, such as aphids.

Potato wart

Serious problem with potatoes, caused by fungal spores that live dormant in soil for many years. Tubers develop large, warty growths, especially around their 'eyes'. Plant only wart-immune varieties and burn infected tubers. It is a notifiable disease (see page 78).

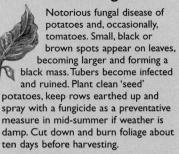

Potato powdery scab

Also known as 'corky scab' and prevalent in wet seasons and on heavy soils. Sometimes, tomato roots are affected. Less frequent than common scab. Raised scabs, with a powdery surface, burst open and release brown, powdery spores. Plant only immune varieties, rotate crops, burn infected tubers and improve soil drainage.

Potato scab

Fungal disease, mainly of potatoes but also affects beetroots, radishes, swedes (rutabagas) and turnips. Potato tubers are attacked while still small, producing scurfy scabs, first somewhat circular, later patchy and spreading. Although unsightly, the flesh is not affected. Use scab-resistant varieties, do not add lime to the soil and plant clean 'seed' potatoes.

Violet root rot

Fungal disease of asparagus, beetroots, carrots, parsnips, potatoes, swedes (rutabagas), turnips and celery. Soil-borne fungus, infesting underground parts, which become covered with purple or violet fungal threads. Pull up and burn infected plants and do not grow root-type crops on the land for four years.

Brown heart

Sometimes known as boron deficiency, a problem with roots of swedes (rutabagas) and, to a lesser degree, turnips. Beetroots are sometimes affected, while boron deficiency on celery occurs as cracks across the stems. If boron is known to be deficient, apply borax, but only in small amounts.

Black rot

Produces black and sunken areas – close to the crown – of stored carrots. Fungus gains entry to roots through damage caused by pests and carelessness when digging roots for storage. Remove and burn infected roots and rotate crops of carrots.

Carrot root rot

Also known as 'Sclerotinia rot', a major disease affecting many plants and usually seen as a soft rot of root crops; problem of stored carrots. Roots become covered in a white, woolly mould. Store only sound and healthy roots and burn infected plants.

DISEASES OF STEMS, LEAVES AND ROOTS OF VEGETABLES (CONTINUED)

Celery leaf spot

Also known as 'celery blight', a seed-borne fungal disease of celery seedlings and mature plants. Appears as brown spots on outer leaflets, then spreads; most destructive in wet weather. Burn seriously infected plants, spray with a fungicide and sow only 'thiram' or 'hot-water' treated seed. Do not plant infected seedlings.

Celery heart rot

Also known as 'bacterial soft rot', it cannot usually be detected until plants are harvested, when centres reveal a wet, slimy, brown rot. Bacteria enter through damage caused by pests or careless cultivation. Burn infected plants.

Lettuce ring spot

Most damaging in cold weather and on winter lettuces. Chicory and endives are also affected. Small, brown-yellow spots on undersides of leaves; their centres dry and fall out. Burn seriously infected leaves, spray with a fungicide, rotate crops and ensure land is well drained.

Beet leaf spots

Disfiguring disease, most prevalent on spinach beet and red beet. Small, somewhat circular, purple-brown spots have pale central areas. Pick off and burn badly affected leaves. Feed plants with a balanced fertilizer and rotate crops.

Spinach blight

Thought to be initiated by cucumber mosaic virus. First, young, inner leaves become yellow and distorted and roll inwards. Outer leaves become limp and yellow and rest on the ground. Some varieties are resistant. Burn infected plants and spray others against insects such as aphids.

Root rots

Several fungal diseases damage roots of plants, including cucumbers, marrows, courgettes (zucchinis), squashes and pumpkins. Black rots are especially damaging, with root systems becoming black. Burn infected plants, avoid wet soil or compost, and always use sterilized compost.

Cucumber mosaic virus

Virus of cucumbers, squashes, marrows, courgettes (zucchinis) and pumpkins. Leaves become puckered and mottled with yellow. Burn all infected plants, avoid touching 'clean' plants afterwards, and spray to control sap-sucking insects such as aphids.

Basal stem rot

Also known as 'cucumber foot rot' and 'soft rot', a bacterial disease that attacks cucumbers, as well as marrows, courgettes (zucchinis), squashes and pumpkins. Bases of stems decay, leaves wilt and stems collapse. Keep the bases of plants dry and dust with a fungicide.

Tomato foot rot

Mainly a disease of seedlings, but may also attack older plants and especially tomatoes in greenhouses. It is encouraged by close, stuffy conditions and badly drained compost or soil. Watering compost and soil with Cheshunt compound helps to prevent infection.

White tip of leeks

Also known as 'leek white tip', it attacks onions and leeks. Tips of leaves assume a waterlogged appearance, turning white and becoming papery. Infection spreads and growth is checked. Burn infected plants, spray with a fungicide and do not grow leeks or onions on the land for three years.

Rusts

Wide range, affecting vegetables including onions, leeks, chives, garlic, asparagus, dwarf and runner beans and broad (fava) beans. On onions, dusty orange spots and blotches appear on leaves. Remove and burn infected leaves and rotate crops.

Smut

Soil-borne disease of onions, leeks, shallots, chives and garlic. Dull spotting or streaking on leaves, which become twisted and thickened. Burn infected plants and do not grow onion-type plants on the same ground for eight or more years.

Onion neck rot

Fungal disease; usually appears on harvested and stored onions. The bulb's neck softens and turns brownish; later, sooty black when spores appear. Bulbs become unusable and the disease spreads. Only store healthy bulbs and regularly inspect those being stored.

Tomato leaf mould

Widespread in greenhouses, but rare outdoors. Upper leaf surfaces become pale and yellow; undersides covered with a pale grey-brown mould. Leaves shrivel. Encouraged by warm, moist conditions. Remove infected leaves and spray with a fungicide. Increase ventilation, especially at night.

Parsnip canker

Shoulders of parsnips become black and rotten. Encouraged by cracking of roots, irregular rainfall, wet weather and high nitrogen or lime-deficient soil. Grow canker-resistant varieties, add lime to the soil, control pests such as carrot fly and sow seeds later than normal.

Onion white rot

Also known as 'mouldy nose'; fungal disease of onions, leeks, shallots, garlic and chives. Foliage turns yellow and wilts and a white or grey fluffy mould appears on the bases of bulbs. Burn diseased plants and do not grow onion-related plants on the same piece of ground for eight years.

SOIL AND ROOT PROBLEMS OF VEGETABLES

Root-knot eelworms

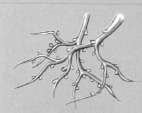

These pernicious pests cause galls and deformation of roots of many vegetables, including lettuces, potatoes, tomatoes, cucumbers, French beans and, occasionally, carrots, beetroot and parsnips. Result in stunted growth, yellowed leaves and wilted plants.

Check the roots for galls. Dig up and burn infected plants and rotate crops, with long intervals.

Cutworms

Larva

Large yellow underwing

These are the caterpillars of various moths, especially turnip moths, heart and dart moths, and large yellow underwing moths (illustrated). The larvae chew stems at ground level, causing wilting and the plant to collapse. In addition to stems, roots (beetroots, turnips, swedes/rutabagas and carrots) and tubers (potatoes) are often attacked. Search out the caterpillars and dust the soil with an insecticide.

Wireworms

Distinctive larvae of the click beetle, or 'skip-jack', which chew roots, stems and tubers. They are most prevalent on land newly cultivated from grassland. Dust the soil with an insecticide. Trapping is possible by shallowly burying cut carrots or potatoes and removing them when congested with wireworms.

Leatherjackets

Fat, legless, greyish-brown grubs, the larvae of the cranefly (daddy-longlegs). Adults lay eggs in the soil, which hatch and the grubs feed on roots. They are especially prevalent on land newly cultivated from grassland. Water the soil with a pesticide and deeply cultivate land in winter when you are preparing it for vegetables.

Millipedes

Both the black and snake millipedes damage plants, feeding on roots, bulbs and tubers, often after initial damage has been caused by slugs and wireworms. In autumn, burn all rubbish and when preparing a new bed deeply cultivate the soil in winter. Dust the soil with a pesticide.

Snails

Similar appetites and natures to slugs. They hide in rubbish and under stones and are especially active at night and during periods of wet and mild weather. Use baits and traps; see pages 6–7 for non-chemical controls.

Slugs

Well-known pests, hiding in the day and feeding at night. They are encouraged by damp conditions, eating roots, bulbs and tubers. Use baits and traps; see pages 6–7 for non-chemical controls.

Cabbage root fly

Attack cabbages, cauliflowers, Brussels sprouts, calabrese, radishes, turnips and swedes (rutabagas). Small, white maggots live in the soil and eat roots, causing leaves to wilt and turn bluish-purple, especially during dry periods. Dust rows of transplants with an insecticide. Alternatively, spray around bases of young plants.

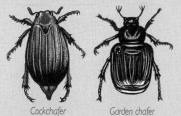

Clubroot

Also known as 'finger-and-toe', it infests roots of cabbages, Brussels sprouts, cauliflowers, swedes (rutabagas) and turnips. Plants wilt, grow slowly and eventually die. Prevalent on acid and badly drained soil. Lift and burn infected plants, add lime to the soil and improve drainage. Dip roots of transplants in a fungicide.

Cockchafer grubs

Cockchafer   *Garden chafer*

Also known as 'May bugs' or 'June bugs', the larvae live in the soil and feed on vegetables' roots and tubers, causing wilting and death. Often seen in land newly converted from pasture. Dig soil in winter, before planting and sowing vegetables in spring and summer. Also use a pesticide.

Woodlice

Grey, hard-coated pests that shelter in damp and shaded positions, where they live on decaying plant material. They also eat seedlings and chew roots. Dust the soil with a pesticide. They are also known as 'pillbugs', 'slaters' and 'sowbugs'.

CULTURAL PROBLEMS OF VEGETABLES

Blossom drop

Affects tomatoes and is usually caused by dry air and insufficient soil moisture. Flower stalks become yellow and snap off at the knuckle, just above the flower. Flowers are not pollinated. Water plants regularly, and mist-spray flowers in the morning. In addition, tapping plants encourages pollination.

Blossom end rot

Circular, leathery, brown patches occur on the fruit's skin at the blossom end (bottom) of tomatoes. Results from a check in soil moisture through irregular watering. Often occurs when tomatoes are in growing-bags. Keep the compost or soil evenly moist, especially when fruits are swelling.

Blotchy ripening

Only parts of tomato fruits ripen, leaving yellow or orange areas. It results from a deficiency of nitrogen or potash. Also caused by high temperatures and inadequate ventilation in greenhouses. Feed plants regularly with a balanced tomato fertilizer, and control greenhouse temperatures.

Bull neck

Also known as 'thick neck', the necks of onions are abnormally broad. Caused by excessively fertile soil and feeding with a high-nitrogen fertilizer. It is encouraged by sowing seeds too deeply. Rectify the above causes, and do not add too much manure to the soil.

Saddleback

Onion bulbs, when harvested, have splits at their bases; these are mostly associated with growing onions from sets (small bulbs), but excessive soil moisture after a drought is also a cause. Do not allow the soil to become dry, especially during dry seasons.

Greenback

Affects tomatoes; areas around stalks remain green, harden and do not ripen. Caused by too little potash and too much sunshine when fruits are ripening. Grow resistant varieties, and shade and ventilate the greenhouse, especially on hot days. Feed plants when ripening.

Blown Brussels sprouts

Individual buttons become leafy and open, and not hard and round. There are several causes, including loose soil when planted, insufficient organic material and lack of water in periods of dry weather. Do not put plants too close together.

Heartless cabbages

Cabbages fail to produce hearts; usually caused by the same conditions that encourage blown Brussels sprouts (see left). Feeding with a balanced fertilizer helps prevent the problem. Always ensure that young plants are firmly planted.

Whiptail

Affects cauliflowers and broccoli, reducing the width of the leaf blade and producing a tail-like appearance. Caused by a deficiency of molybdenum on acid soil. Before planting or sowing, check that the soil is not acid.

Dry set

Occurs on tomato fruitlets when they reach the size of a match-head. They stop developing and remain as a small, bulbous head. Caused by a dry atmosphere during pollination. Mist-spray plants daily (morning and evening) to avoid this problem.

Fanging

Occurs with carrots, and occasionally parsnips, when roots fork. The problem is initiated by adding fresh manure to the soil just before sowing seeds, shallow soil preparation and stony conditions. If possible, grow carrots on land not manured in the previous year.

Tip burn

Affects lettuces, when edges of leaves appear to be scorched. Encouraged by sudden dryness in the soil, especially in periods of warm weather during spring and early summer. Ensure that the soil remains evenly moist, especially during periods of low rainfall.

Bolting

Premature flowering and production of seeds by vegetables such as beetroot, brassicas, lettuces, onions and spinach. Reasons include too-early sowing and loose soil. Always firm the soil before sowing or planting.

Split fruits

Problem with tomatoes; fruits split laterally and leave wide gaps. Occurs outdoors and in greenhouses and is encouraged by excessive watering after the soil has become dry. Keep the soil evenly moist throughout the summer.

Hollow fruits

Occurs with tomatoes; fruits do not swell, but sink and have hollow centres when cut open. Caused by ineffective pollination (through air being too dry, cold or hot) or lack of potash. Control ventilation in greenhouses to prevent rapid temperature fluctuations.

Sun scald

Problem with tomatoes in greenhouses with high light intensity; papery-skinned depressions appear on the sides of fruits, especially those facing the glass. Paint the glass with 'shading' and regularly mist-spray plants, but not at midday when the sun is at its strongest.

Hollow heart

Problem with large potato tubers, when the centres (revealed if cut open) are hollow. Encouraged by excessively wet weather after dry periods, and usually only noticed when potatoes rot in store. Keep the soil adequately and evenly moist during dry periods.

Buckeye rot

Problem with tomatoes; soil-borne spores splash onto low trusses and form circles around a grey spot on unripe fruits. Burn infected fruits, water carefully and tie up lower trusses. Forming a peat mulch around plants helps to prevent spores splashing on them.

Carrot splitting

Roots become deeply cracked along their lengths; caused by excessive watering after periods of dry weather. Do not store these carrots, as they encourage the presence of decay. You can reduce the risk of splitting by adding well-decomposed compost to the soil; do not use fresh compost or farmyard manure. Keep the soil moist, especially during periods of drought.

Potato splitting

Deep cracks appear on tubers; usually caused by excessive watering after periods of dry weather. Do not store cracked potatoes as they encourage decay. Keep plants evenly watered throughout their growing period, especially when the weather is hot and the soil is at risk of becoming dry.

Plants in homes and greenhouses

I ndoor, greenhouse and conservatory plants are often at less risk from pests and diseases than those growing outdoors, because large concentrations of similar outdoor plants encourage the build-up of pests and diseases. You should still be alert for some pests and diseases, however. The 'plus' factor is that, if you always use clean compost, pots and seed-trays (flats), plants growing in pots indoors will not suffer in the same way from soil pests as those growing outdoors.

Are indoor plants at risk?

PESTS OF PLANTS IN HOMES AND GREENHOUSES

Cyclamen mites

Especially troublesome indoors on a wide range of plants, including cyclamens, begonias, gloxinias and pelargoniums. They infest the undersides of leaves, causing bronzing on upper surfaces; leaves and flowers become stunted and distorted. Destroy infected leaves and use an acaricide (see page 78).

Aphids (greenfly)

Insects that pierce leaves, stems, flower buds and flowers, sucking sap and causing debilitation. They transmit viruses and excrete honeydew, which encourages the presence of sooty mould (see page 70). Spray plants with a systemic insecticide.

Chrysanthemum leaf miners

Infest cinerarias as well as chrysanthemums, tunnelling into leaves and causing disfigure-ment. Tunnels are often merged. Pick off and destroy affected leaves. Once established, controls are difficult but spraying with a systemic insecticide helps to reduce their spread.

Fungus gnats

Also known as 'mushroom fly'. Small, black flies (themselves harmless) lay eggs in compost; these result in white, legless larvae that normally feed on organic material in compost but occasionally attack roots of plants. Drench the soil in an insecticide.

Mealy bugs

Small, white, mealy-covered, woodlouse-like pests that cluster on stems and under leaves. They suck sap, excreting honeydew, which encourages the presence of sooty mould (see page 70). Wipe off with a cotton bud dipped in methylated spirits. Alternatively, spray with a systemic insecticide.

Earwigs

Widespread pest, sometimes seen in old greenhouses and conservatories. They mainly feed at night, chewing leaves and flowers and giving them a ragged appearance. During the day they hide under pots and greenhouse staging. Pick off and destroy them, or use a pesticide.

Eelworms

Microscopic, thin and transparent, soil-living pests that sometimes invade houseplants. Several types, some causing corky swellings on roots, others invading stems and leaves. Destroy plants, discard compost (not onto a compost heap), and buy eelworm-free plants.

Caterpillars

Larvae (caterpillars) of moths and butterflies may attack plants in greenhouses and conservatories, chewing holes in leaves and, occasionally, flowers. Pick them off and spray with a contact insecticide. They are rarely present on plants indoors, unless introduced on infected plants.

Scale insects

Several races of scale (usually small, brown discs) infest stems and undersides of leaves, usually in greenhouses rather than indoors. When they are young and at the 'crawler' stage, scales are easily wiped off with a damp cloth. Alternatively, destroy plants or spray with a systemic insecticide.

Vine weevils

Pernicious insects; adult beetles chew leaves, while legless, white, brown-headed larvae feed on roots, corms and tubers. Pick off and destroy beetles. Plants with roots affected by larvae wilt; either discard plants or drench soil in an insecticide.

Red spider mites

Minute, eight-legged, spider-like pests, usually red, feed on the undersides of leaves, sucking sap, and create light bronzing above. They sometimes form webbing. Regularly mist-spray plants and spray with a systemic insecticide at first sign of attack. Destroy seriously affected plants.

Woodlice

Sometimes seen in damp, shaded and old greenhouses and conservatories. They are grey and hard-coated, mainly feeding at night and chewing roots, stems and leaves. Remove all hiding places and spray with a pesticide. They are also known as 'pillbugs', 'slaters' and 'sowbugs'.

Greenhouse whitefly

They resemble minute, white, mealy-covered moths, which suck sap, mainly on the undersides of leaves. They excrete honeydew, which encourages the presence of sooty mould (see page 70). Spray with a contact or systemic insecticide as soon as they are seen.

Greenhouse thrips

Small, black, fly-like insects that flutter and jump from one plant to another. They suck sap from leaves and flowers, creating silvery streaks. When feeding, they produce small, red and brown globules of liquid on the undersides of leaves. Spray with a contact or systemic insecticide.

Cockroaches

These are nature's survivors and are sometimes seen in old, warm green-houses and conservatories. They feed on many plants, roots, stems, leaves and flowers. Clear away all rubbish and use traps and baits. They are notoriously difficult to eradicate.

DISEASES OF PLANTS IN HOMES AND GREENHOUSES

Corky scab

Sometimes known as 'oedema' and 'dropsy', hard, corky growths appear on undersides of leaves; seen on cacti (see page 75) and other houseplants. Caused by excessive watering, along with low light and high temperatures. Water less frequently, reduce temperatures and move plants to better light.

Rust

Range of rusts that affect many houseplants, including zonal pelargoniums, where circular clusters of raised, rusty-brown pustules appear on undersides of leaves. Remove and burn infected plants or spray with a rust fungicide. Do not take cuttings from infected plants.

Leaf spot

Range of bacterial or fungal diseases, affecting plants such as *Dieffenbachia*, *Citrus* and *Dracaena*; moist, brown spots appear on leaves. Remove and burn infected leaves, spray with a systemic fungicide, keep the leaves dry and keep the compost only slightly moist.

Crown and stem rots

Several fungal diseases infect plants in pots, either at their bases or on stems. These parts turn soft, brown and rotten. Excess watering, cool temperatures and lack of ventilation usually cause these problems. Seriously infected plants are best discarded.

Black leg

Infects cuttings, often of pelargoniums but also of other houseplants. Base of cutting turns black and soft. Caused by a fungal disease but encouraged by waterlogged and compacted compost. Burn seriously infected cuttings and use sterilized compost.

Sooty mould

Fungal disease that lives on honeydew excreted by aphids and other sap-sucking pests. Black fungus is, at first, patchy, then completely covers the leaf, making it unsightly and blocking pores. Wipe away small areas with a damp cloth and control sap-sucking pests.

Viruses

Several viruses affect plants growing in pots indoors, in greenhouses and in conservatories. Leaves assume pale or yellow patches or mottling and the plant becomes stunted and distorted. Burn infected plants and spray against sap-sucking insects.

Grey mould (Botrytis)

A fluffy, grey mould covers leaves, stems, buds and flowers. It is encouraged by still and humid air. Fungal spores enter plants through cuts. Use sterilized compost and improve ventilation. Remove infected plants and use Cheshunt compound.

Root rots

Caused by several different fungal diseases, when roots of plants such as begonias and saintpaulias decay and totally or partially cease to function. The first sign is plants wilting, followed by browning; usually a result of excessive watering. Discard any seriously affected plants.

Powdery mildew

Fungal disease, producing a white, powdery coating of spores on stems and leaves (usually on both surfaces) and spreading to flowers. Remove and burn badly affected parts and spray with a systemic fungicide. Improve air circulation around plants.

Damping off

Fungal disease of seedlings, when they collapse at compost level. Excessively wet compost, congested seedlings, compacted compost and high temperatures encourage it. Always use sterilized compost and provide good ventilation. Water seedlings with Cheshunt compound.

Anthracnose

Sunken brown-black spots appear on the leaves. Leaf tips are also affected. The disease is encouraged by damp conditions and excessive warmth. Remove all infected leaves and use a systemic fungicide. Do not mist-spray plants and keep the compost slightly dry.

Orchids

Are orchids especially at risk?

Several pests and diseases can cause trouble on orchids, but you should have few problems if you buy only 'clean' plants from reputable sources and treat any symptoms quickly. However, it is essential that you only use chemicals that are specifically recommended for orchids, and always thoroughly inspect plants when they are bought. Prevention is much better and easier than trying to control established outbreaks on orchids.

GREENHOUSE HYGIENE

Greenhouses that have become neglected often harbour pests, such as the following:

- **Cockroaches** are difficult to eradicate once established and have an appetite for most plants. They mostly feed at night; infestations can usually be kept under control by using traps and baits. Remove all rubbish. Although it is claimed that cockroaches eat anything, some experts say that they dislike putty and cucumber!

- **Millipedes** feed on roots and other parts at or below compost level. They are slower-moving than centipedes, which have one pair of legs on each segment; millipedes have two pairs on each segment. Remove all rubbish, use baits and dust with a pesticide.

- **Woodlice** are discouraged by thoroughly cleaning the greenhouse and removing all rubbish. Dust 'at risk' areas with a pesticide.

PESTS OF ORCHIDS

Aphids

Often seen in clusters around shoots and on leaves and flowers, sucking sap, spreading viruses and causing puckering and pale areas. They also excrete honeydew, which encourages the presence of sooty mould (see page 73). Use a systemic insecticide.

Mealy bugs

Small, white, mealy-covered, woodlice-like pests that cluster around leaf-joints and stems and under leaves. Wipe off small groups with a damp cloth or moist cotton bud. Severe infestations are difficult to eradicate and are best treated with a systemic insecticide.

Greenhouse thrips

Small, black, fly-like insects that flutter from one plant to another. They feed on flowers and leaves by piercing the tissue and sucking sap, causing silvery mottling. Bad infestations produce stunted and unsightly plants. As soon as they are noticed, spray with a systemic insecticide.

Scale insects

Resemble small, brown discs, usually attached to the undersides of leaves and especially along veins. When young and at the 'crawler' stage, they can be wiped away with a damp cloth or moist cotton bud. Use a systemic insecticide for severe infestations – they are difficult to eradicate.

Weevils

Pernicious, beetle-like pests that feed on plants, mainly at night. The creamy-white larvae have mouth parts adapted to eating roots. Chewed leaves are easily seen, but the first indication of larvae is when the foliage wilts. Spray the foliage and drench the compost in an insecticide.

Red spider mites

Minute, eight-legged, spider-like, brownish-red or straw-coloured pests that cause upper surfaces to become speckled with yellow blotches. Severe infestations are very unsightly and cause leaves to fall off. Webbing might also be present. Spray the plant with a systemic insecticide.

DISEASES OF ORCHIDS

Often, diseases in orchids go unnoticed until well established. Therefore it is essential to check plants regularly, above and under leaves and around the plant's base. The flowers can also be affected. Here are a few diseases that may damage orchids. If your orchid is unhealthy and growth is old and stunted, do not expect it to flower profusely – or even at all. Check that the plant is getting good light and does not need to be repotted because its roots are congested.

Petal blight

Fungal disease that attacks a wide range of plants with soft tissue. In greenhouses, it is mainly caused by high humidity and results in dark brown or black spots, with pinkish edges on the petals. In orchids, it mainly occurs in early autumn, on flowers of *Cattleya* and *Phalaenopsis* species.

Immediately flowers are seen with this problem, remove and burn them, and ensure that night-time humidity is not high. In cool situations, provide additional warmth in autumn.

Sooty mould

Black fungus that grows on honeydew excreted by aphids and other sap-sucking pests. The black fungus spreads across leaves and other parts. Wipe it from leaves with a soft, damp cloth, then rinse with clean water. Then, to prevent this mould reappearing, spray with a systemic insecticide to kill sap-sucking insects.

Brown spot

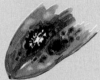

Known in North America as 'brown rot', it is a bacterial disease that attacks *Phalaenopsis*, *Paphiopedilum* and *Cattleya* orchids. Early signs of infection are soft, watery areas on a leaf's surface, which soon become black or brown, then spread further. Specifically, on *Cattleya* orchids it is usually limited to older leaves, appearing as sunken black spots; on *Phalaenopsis* orchids it usually starts as a soft, water-soaked lesion, which later becomes black or brown.

Infected areas should be cut out with a sharp, clean knife, and burned to prevent infection spreading. Dust cut surfaces with a fungicide. Once established in a collection of orchids, it is difficult to eradicate.

Rust

Unsightly disease and especially prevalent on *Cattleya*, *Epidendrum*, *Laelia* and *Oncidium* orchids. Orange-yellow patches develop on the lower leaf surfaces, while the upper sides reveal yellow-green, mottled areas directly above the patches.

It is difficult to eradicate rust, and severely infected plants are best isolated or burned. Always carefully inspect new plants.

Viruses

Their initial purpose is not to kill plants but to use them as hosts. Once a plant is infected, it is extremely difficult to eradicate a virus. Eventually, infected plants have to be burned. Viruses are spread either through infected tissue being propagated or through sap-sucking insects such as aphids. It is therefore essential to prevent insect infestation and to buy only healthy plants.

Cacti and other succulents

Are they pest- and disease-resistant?

Cacti and other succulents are among the most popular plants for homes and conservatories and, although relatively trouble-free, there are some pests and diseases, as well as cultural problems, that can seriously damage them. These plants are able to withstand periods of drought, but they are sometimes put at risk from rotting or soft-tissue decay when given too much water. Therefore, always ensure that excess water can readily drain away.

CACTI OR SUCCULENT?

Cacti belong exclusively to the Cactaceae family and are characterized by having areoles (resembling small pin-cushions) from which develop spines, short hooks or long and woolly hairs. Another characteristic of the cactus family is that, with the exception of *Pereskia* and young *Opuntia* plants, none of them have normal leaves. Additionally, with one exception – the *Pereskia* – all cacti are succulents and have the ability to store water in their fleshy leaves and stems. The range of non-cacti succulents is wide and includes popular houseplants, such as *Echeveria*, *Lithops* and *Sedum*.

Cacti can be divided into two groups: desert types, whose natural environment is the semi-desert regions of the American continent, and forest types which come from the forest regions of tropical America. An exception is *Rhipsalis baccifera*, which is native to Africa, Madagascar and Sri Lanka, as well as America.

PESTS OF CACTI AND OTHER SUCCULENTS

Mealy bugs

Small, white, mealy-covered, woodlice-like pests cluster on stems and leaves (where present), sucking sap, excreting honeydew and encouraging sooty mould. Minor infestations can be cleared with a moist cotton bud or small brush. Alternatively, use a systemic insecticide.

Spider mites

Occasionally infest cacti and succulents, especially if the weather is hot and the air dry. These minute, spider-like pests can seriously infest plants and often result in fine webbing. Mist-spraying deters them. Use a systemic insecticide as soon as they are noticed.

Root mealy bugs

Pernicious pests, resembling ordinary mealy bugs and infesting roots. They cluster in colonies, chewing roots and causing plants to wilt and, eventually, to die. Drench the compost with a systemic insecticide. Infestations are worse when compost is dry.

Cochineal scale

Cochineal is a traditional red dye of pre-Hispanic Mexico and has been employed to colour clothing and foods including sausages, pies, dried fish, candies and jams. It has also been used as a colourant for lipstick and rouge. This dye is obtained from female cochineal scale insects, which spend their lives feeding on *Opuntia* spp., or Prickly Pear cacti.

In the late 1700s the Spanish monopoly on cochineal production was broken when cactus pads, together with the scale insects, were smuggled to Haiti. Later, they spread to South America, India, North Africa and Europe; this is why this Mexican cactus is now widely seen growing in other countries.

Cactus scale

Often seen on old or neglected cacti. Several types of scale infest cacti, but it is usually seen as small, brown discs on stems and undersides of leaves, especially along the veins. At the 'crawler' stage, they can be cleared with a damp cotton bud. Alternatively, use a systemic insecticide.

Root-knot eelworms

Sometimes pests of greenhouse and conservatory plants occasionally infest compost in which cacti and succulents are growing, causing corky swellings on roots. Burn plants, discard compost in a place where it cannot reinfect other plants and buy eelworm-free plants.

DISEASES OF CACTI AND OTHER SUCCULENTS

Crown gall

Infests a wide range of garden plants and some cacti; in their native areas, cacti such as *Carnegiea gigantea* are seriously infected. The spongy galls are encouraged by damage to stems through rough handling and insect damage. Always use sterilized compost.

Root rot (tuber rot)

Serious problem; roots decay, causing yellowing, wilting and total collapse. Usually results from excessively wet compost, which excludes air. If only a slight problem exists, remove the pot, wrap the rootball in absorbent paper (kitchen towel) until it dries and then replace the rootball in a clean pot.

Other diseases and physiological problems

- **Fusarium rot:** Young segments of *Opuntia* spp. become dark grey or black. Usually, the infected area is initially dry, brittle and clearly defined. Later, these lesions decay, developing brown blotches and irregular shapes. It is often seen at the bases of segments. Prevention involves avoiding congestion and syringing plants (which spreads infection from plant to plant), and using a fungicide.

- **Pad decay:** Affects stems and branches; caused by a fungus that enters the plant through damaged tissue and is encouraged by high temperatures. Cut out diseased parts and spray with a fungicide.

- **Sun scald:** Problem with *Opuntia* spp. At first, spots on the segments are distinctively zoned, the affected area greyish-brown and slightly cracked. Later, damaged areas turn reddish-brown and pads die. Some initial damage usually enables diseases to enter the plant. The only solution is to provide opuntias with slight shade.

- **Viruses:** These pernicious, microscopic particles invade some cacti, especially *Epiphyllum* spp., causing yellow or, occasionally, purple spots. They also affect the flowers, which may develop striped and broken colours. Viruses are notoriously difficult to eradicate – if not impossible. Therefore, always buy clean plants. Burn infected plants.

Stem rot

A rapidly progressing rot, which begins with well-defined yellow lesions, later dark brown. Sometimes, entire plants collapse and die with a few days. The fungus enters plants through wounds, especially in young plants. Discard serious affected plants, use sterilized compost and spray with a fungicide.

Anthracnose of Opuntia

Fungal disease that enters its host and spreads rapidly throughout the segment, causing a moist, light brown rot that slowly becomes black. Cut out affected pads and use a fungicide. Always use sterilized compost to reduce risk of infection.

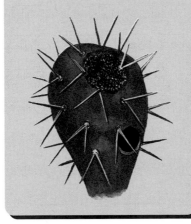

CULTURAL PROBLEMS

Corky scab

Sometimes known as 'oedema', it produces rusty or corky spots on stems of many cacti; the disease especially affects *Opuntia* and *Epiphyllum* spp. Usually, only young stems remain free from the problem. Decrease humidity and increase the amount of light; however, avoid extra strong light.

Bud fall

The premature dropping of buds and stunting of growth. It is usually caused by lack of nourishment, including an excess of nitrogen. Dry compost, the use of very cold water when syringing plants and rapid temperature changes can also cause buds to drop off.

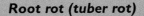

Corky scab

Glassiness

Dark green, translucent spots occur on stems and, if pressed and crushed, rapidly turn black. Severe attacks may kill shoots above the spots; mild attacks sometimes initiate corky layers or spots which isolate diseased tissue. Increase the amount of light and decrease humidity.

Wilting

Both insufficient and excessive soil moisture cause plants to wilt. If the compost is dry, give more water. However, excessive watering causes plants to collapse and, eventually, the roots and stems to decay. It is usually a problem in winter when plants are not active and the temperature is low. If the growing pot is in a saucer, rather than a cache pot, it is easier to see if water remains at the plant's base.

Checklist for 'green' solutions

ORNAMENTAL PLANTS (BEDDING PLANTS, TREES AND SHRUBS)

- Grease bands attached to stems of half-standard and standard roses prevent ants reaching honeydew excreted by aphids and other sap-sucking insects.
- Traps baited with orange peel, lettuce, cabbage leaves, cucumber rind and heaps of moist bran help to entrap slugs and snails.
- Inverted pots packed with straw and spiked on bamboo canes entrap earwigs. Tip out the earwigs each morning and burn them.
- Shaking branches of ornamental pear and cherry trees, as well as rhododendrons, dislodges weevils; place a sheet of white paper or canvas on the ground beneath branches and jar or shake branches. Capture and burn the weevils.
- Hand-picking pests, from slugs and snails to caterpillars, helps to reduce their numbers.
- Sprinkling broken eggshells around plants helps to deter slugs and snails. Sharp-edged shingle can also be used.

Broken eggshells scattered around tender plants help to deter slugs and snails from reaching succulent stems and leaves.

VEGETABLES AND HERBS

Covering onion plants with horticultural fleece helps to prevent egg-laying around young plants.

- Traps formed of large pieces of carrot or potato tubers slightly buried in the ground attract wireworms and millipedes; later, remove and burn.
- Cabbage root fly barriers – placing a piece of carpet underlay (padding), 13–15 cm (5–6 in) square, around a cabbage or other brassica plant immediately after planting helps to prevent these flies laying eggs around plants. On one of the sides, cut a slit to the centre, so that the underlay fits snugly around the plant's stem.
- Blackfly are repelled by both *Satureja hortensis* and *S. montana* (Summer and Winter Savory) planted alongside susceptible vegetables, such as bean crops.
- Carrot root fly can be deterred by growing plants with strong aromas, such as *Allium sativum* (Garlic), alongside rows of carrots.
- Eelworms can be deterred by plantings of *Tagetes* spp.
- Onions can be protected from onion fly by covering plants with horticultural fleece; this prevents the female flies laying eggs near the bases of plants.

Lawns

To control leatherjackets in lawns, soak affected areas with water and cover overnight with black plastic sheeting. The leatherjackets rise to the surface and can then either be swept off or left to the attention of birds.

GREENHOUSES

- Sacking placed on the floor or staging entraps earwigs and vine weevil beetles. Each morning, remove, shake out and burn these pests.
- Traps formed of partially scooped-out potatoes will lure woodlice in greenhouses (place traps under staging) and frames outdoors. They are also ideal for old orchid houses, where pests are perhaps entrenched.
- Sunken jam-jars baited with sugar and beer are ideal for capturing cockroaches.
- Yellow decoy traps, coated in a sticky, non-drying glue, attract aphids. There are no insecticides involved and beneficial insects are not harmed. These traps can also be used outdoors.

Yellow, sticky traps in a greenhouse will attract and trap troublesome pests, such as whitefly.

TREE FRUITS

Bands of sacking or corrugated card rolled around trunks of fruit trees help to trap larvae of the codling moth.

- Grease bands – place them around trunks of trees in early autumn to capture the wingless females of the winter moth, the mottled umber moth and the March moth.
- Corrugated cardboard – rolled pieces of sacking or specially prepared bands of corrugated paper, when placed either in the crotch of trees or around the stems of fruit and ornamental trees, capture the apple blossom weevil and larvae of the codling moth.

GENERAL REMINDERS

- Clear away all rubbish that could harbour pests and diseases. During autumn, rake out and burn rubbish from hedge bases.
- Keep plants free from weeds – they provide a sanctuary for pests and reduce the circulation of air around plants, encouraging the presence of diseases.
- Use deep soil preparation – when preparing new beds, deep soil cultivation exposes soil pests, such as cockchafer grubs, wireworms and cutworms, to birds and frost. It also encourages deep roots and, therefore, plants that are better able to tolerate drought and withstand sap-sucking pests such as aphids.
- Install land drains – excessive soil moisture encourages the presence of pests such as slugs, snails, millipedes and leatherjackets.

- Shallowly hoe around plants throughout summer; this helps to deter soil pests.
- Annually rotate vegetable crops to prevent the build-up of pests and diseases.
- Birds can soon ravage plants, but robins and wagtails eat raspberry grubs, nuthatches eat codling moths, and starlings feed on wireworms.

Further information

Non-chemical ways to prevent and control pests and diseases are detailed on pages 4–5, while a range of beneficial insects is featured on pages 6–7.

Glossary

Abdomen The rear part of an insect, which contains the digestive system and sex organs.

Acaricide Chemical that is used to kill mites.

Antennae Feelers attached to the head of an insect.

Bacterial disease Plant disease that is caused by bacteria, which are microscopic, single-celled organisms that develop within the cells of plants. Examples of bacterial diseases are potato black leg, crown gall and gladiolus scab.

Beneficial insects These help to control plant-damaging insects and other pests. Examples of beneficial creatures include frogs, toads and hedgehogs, which feed on many pests. Many birds also help in reducing the numbers of pests, but this has to be balanced by their harmful activities, which include tearing leaves, damaging buds and disturbing seeds.

Biological controls Controlling and preventing pests by the use of predators, parasites and diseases.

Biting pests Insects and other pests that bite or chew various parts of plants, such as leaves, stems and flowers.

Brassica Plant that belongs to the cabbage family, which includes Brussels sprouts, broccoli, cauliflowers, turnips and swedes (rutabagas).

Caterpillar The larva of a butterfly or moth.

Certified stock Plants that are guaranteed to be of a specified quality and free from viruses.

Chrysalis Term applies to the pupa or inactive stage in the life cycle of many insects, especially of butterflies and moths.

Cocoon Protective case, of silk or other materials, formed by various kinds of larvae for protection while they change into pupae.

Companion planting Growing plants in association with each other in order to reduce pest and disease attack. For example, strong-smelling plants, such as *Allium sativum* (Garlic), help to cloak the presence of susceptible plants from plant-damaging insects.

Crop rotation Usually refers to vegetables, when different types of plants are rotated on a three- or four-year cycle. This helps prevent the build-up of pests and diseases.

Cultivar Plant produced in cultivation and indicating a 'cultivated variety'. Earlier, all variations, whether produced naturally in the wild or in cultivation, were known as 'varieties'. However, as the term 'variety' has been known to gardeners for many decades, it is still frequently used.

Cultural problem Also known as a physiological disorder, it is initiated or encouraged by environmental factors or faulty cultivation.

Dusting Method of applying chemicals to plants.

Elytra Horny wing cases – a term commonly applied to the wing cases of beetles.

Feelers Correctly termed palpi; small appendages on the lower jaws and lower lips of some insects.

Frass Excrement that is often seen around holes through which insects have passed.

Fumigation Used in greenhouses to control pests and diseases. Correctly it refers to 'smokes', but is also applied to aerosols.

Fungal (or fungus) diseases Most fungal diseases of plants are parasitic and feed on host plants, which invariably suffer. The main body of a fungus consists of either single cells or a mass of branching threads known as the mycelium.

Fungicide Chemical that is used to control plant diseases, such as mildews and rusts.

Grease bands Used to encircle the trunks of fruit trees to prevent insects climbing them. For example, they are used to prevent the wingless female adults of the winter moth climbing trunks.

Honeydew Sweet excretions, produced by insects such as aphids, mealy bugs and scale insects, which suck sap from plants. The honeydew encourages the presence of ants as well as sooty mould, which is a fungal problem.

Host plant Plant on which insects and fungal diseases live; it is usually taken to mean native plants that enable insects and diseases to overwinter. Diseases such as rusts often complete their life cycle by living on two or more plants. This also applies to insects such as black bean aphids.

Hypha (plural hyphae) Fine, thread-like material of which fungus is formed.

Insecticidal sticks Small sticks that can be inserted into plants in pots indoors or in greenhouses and conservatories to kill insects.

Insecticide Chemical that is used to kill insect pests.

Larva (plural larvae) Stage in an insect's life, immediately after hatching from an egg. Maggots of flies, as well as caterpillars of butterflies and moths, are all larvae.

Mandibles Upper jaws, positioned horizontally opposite each other and beneath the upper lip.

Midge Small, gnat-like fly.

Mite Microscopic pest with eight legs; it resembles a small spider, and the best-known one is the red spider mite.

Nematicide Pesticide used to control nematodes (eelworms).

Nematode Microscopic worm-like creature that infects leaves, stems and roots of some plants.

Notifiable diseases A few diseases are pernicious and spreading, and if they occur their presence must be reported to the appropriate government department.

Nymph Young, immature, usually wingless insect that is similar to the adult form. It has an incomplete life cycle and does not pass through the usual stages of larva and pupa to reach the adult stage.

Organic gardening Growing plants without the use of synthetic or non-organic materials.

Organic pest control Preventing and controlling pests without the need to use synthetic or non-organic chemicals.

Oviparous Producing eggs.

Ovipositor Sexual part, via which female insects lay their eggs.

Parasite Organism that lives and feeds upon another organism.

Parthenogenesis Development of an egg without fertilization. Several insects, including aphids, are able to produce further generations without the need for fertilization.

Pesticide Chemical that kills both insects and other pests of plants.

Physiological disorder See Cultural problem.

Proboscis The mouthpart of a sucking insect, such as greenfly. It forms a narrow tube for piercing tissue and then sucking plant juices. It also enables an insect to inject plants with saliva, which is often contaminated with viruses.

Prolegs Sucker-like feet, enabling caterpillars and other larvae to hold firmly to a leaf or twig, or any other surface they are clambering over.

Pupa Stage in an insect's development when it is dormant and resting. After a larva has stopped feeding, it passes through several stages and develops into a pupa. Later, an adult insect emerges from the pupal case.

Pupal case The protective covering around a pupa.

Resistant plants Describes those plants that have a natural resistance to pests and diseases.

Rust Form of fungus that results in rust-red or brown spots and patches on plants, especially leaves and stems. Some rust fungi complete their life cycle on one particular species of plant, while others have two hosts for differing stages of their development.

Seed dressings When seeds are mixed with, or coated in, insecticides and fungicides to prevent or reduce the risk of damage from pests or diseases.

Sprays Method of applying chemicals, in greenhouses as well as in the garden.

Sucking pests Pests that pierce the tissue of leaves, stems and flowers and extract sap.

Systemic Describes insecticides and fungicides that are absorbed by plants and carried in the sap to all parts of the plant. These parts become toxic to insects and fungi.

Thorax The part of an insect's body between the abdomen and the head. The insect's wings and legs are attached to it.

Variety See Cultivar.

Vector Carrier of either a disease or a virus.

Virus diseases Viruses are complex, microscopic, living organisms that live in the sap of plants and produce symptoms such as distortion and mottling of the leaves; usually, growth is stunted. Viruses are often spread by sap-sucking insects.

Viviparous Producing living young.

Weevil Type of beetle, with a long, funnel-like snout.

Winter-wash Chemical spray applied in winter to some fruit and ornamental trees and shrubs.

Index

Photographs by AG&G Books.